Healed *for* Life

A STORY OF REDEMPTION

CYNTHIA WENZ

WITH *NEW YORK TIMES* BESTSELLER DAVID GREGORY

LUCIDBOOKS

Healed for Life
A Story of Redemption
Copyright © 2017 by Cynthia Wenz

Published by Lucid Books in Houston, TX.
www.LucidBooksPublishing.com

ISBN-10: 1632961067
ISBN-13: 9781632961068
eISBN-10: 1632961520
eISBN-13: 9781632961525

Special Sales: Most Lucid Books titles are available in special quantity discounts. Custom imprinting or excerpting can also be done to fit special needs. Contact Lucid Books at info@lucidbookspublishing.com.

This book is dedicated to my father, Peter D. Sisto, who was led to salvation in Jesus by my son Roman Peter Sisto Wenz.

I love you, Pop—you are the best dad in the world. You made a way for us, and we all love you for it. You married the best woman in the world who is wholly devoted to your treasured family. Rest in peace—your legacy is undying love of family, and I pray it is passed on, influencing many generations for Life.

Love,

Sissy

TABLE OF CONTENTS

PROLOGUE: WHY THIS BOOK?

I wrote this book for two reasons. First, I want those who read my story to know the redemption and healing that is available in Jesus Christ.

I know what it's like to lie on the abortionist's table because I've been there. Not once, not twice, but three times. I grew up a teenager in a broken home, looking for love in all the wrong places. I know how overwhelming it is to face an unintended pregnancy when you're 15. I know how frightening it is to have a father who struggles with alcoholism and abuse. I know how devastating it can be to wreck a man's marriage.

And I also know, as heartbreaking as my past may have been, that God can heal.

You may feel like no one else has been through the trials you've experienced, but I can humbly assure you that you're not alone. This book is about finding redemption in the only place it can be found. Its purpose is to magnify Christ through the sharing of my story. It's a story of God's incredible, redeeming love that brought healing to my heart.

And it's a story of how God commissioned me with the simple task of sharing my journey of pain and healing, so that others can experience the healing that Christ has given me.

This book is about saying *yes* to healthy relationships, *yes* to informed decisions, and *yes* to the Savior who asks that we allow Him to cleanse, restore, and renew us.

Second, I write this book to provide some insight into how I think we can approach the subject of abortion in a fresh, healthy, loving way, and how we can dramatically reduce abortion in our time.

When we talk about the subject of abortion, we must learn how to have candid, civil, productive dialogue. Public discussion and debate today, as it has for 40-plus years, is nothing but an ongoing sparring match of clichéd verbal jabs. The pro-life and pro-choice arguments are pretty much the same tired comments repeated over and over again. And it's disgusting that they're adopted and repeated based on a person's allegiance to a political party, with little connection to what's really at stake.

My point of view is not shaped by political allegiance. I have no political axe to grind. In my life, I have been:

- A mother
- A wife
- A TV producer
- A CEO
- A volunteer counselor to women experiencing unplanned pregnancies
- A counselor to women who have had abortions

But most importantly, I'm a woman who chose to have three abortions.

So I know what this is all about. I know the fears and anxieties a young woman faces. I know how overwhelmed a woman can feel. I know what it's like to be pregnant by a man who won't take on the father's role. I know the reasons why a woman chooses to have an abortion. I've lived them.

This book is intended to give you an up close and personal—and honest—look at what a woman faces in those circumstances. It is also intended to help women understand what information is needed in those circumstances. Because women, even teenage girls, can make informed decisions—if they have the information they need.

You may be in a difficult circumstance at the moment. I have been there. But life is not over. Your pathway can be up. Your future can be bright. You haven't thrown it away. And God is not finished with you. Not by a long shot.

Despite a painful background, made much more painful by my own choices, today I am whole. I am well. I am content. I am blessed. I look back with peace and forgiveness and am not triggered by the past—a past that once controlled me and almost drove me to the grave.

I am Cynthia Wenz, and I am healed for life! I am married to a rock solid man of God who graciously, lovingly journeyed with me into and through my healing. I am a mother of three amazing young men who endured the healing journey. I have seen the gift of adoption, both mine as a daughter grafted in to God's family, and my son Roman's adoption by my husband, Chris Wenz, Roman's daddy.

As a young girl, I was known as Cindy Sisto, and my life was a series of predictable statistics. Who wants to be a statistic, let alone the banner of all statistics? When a woman terminates a pregnancy in her teens, she typically repeats that, often more than once. I did. If a young woman is told that it is her body and she can terminate to keep her life's possibilities open without consequences, she will likely terminate. I did when I was 15. And 19. And 29. If a woman is told she can have complete sexual freedom without paying a price, she has a one in four chance of contracting a sexually transmitted disease. I contracted them again, and again, and again. I was the stinkin' statistic.

But then, life happened. My life became God's story of redemption. It hurt like hell along the way, but it's a story of healing. It starts inside a place of deep healing in God. It's about what is possible through that redemption that He didn't just make available to me, but to everyone who has experienced life's pain. Some people choose to get stuck in the pain and construct their lives there. I have simply chosen to walk in the fullness of God's redemption, and it has made all the difference. None of us has to get stuck.

I hope the story of what He has done in my life can be a source of great strength and encouragement to you. Let's get started!

Cynthia Wenz
Houston, Texas
July 2017

CHAPTER ONE

AT THE CAPITOL: PART 1

I'm nervous. It's not often that you get the chance to testify before a committee of the Texas State Legislature—not to mention a live audience at my back—and my stomach is in knots.

A few weeks earlier, I had received a call from the director of a prominent pro-life organization in Texas. She wanted to know if I would be willing to testify at the State Capitol regarding a new sonogram bill.

As she described, House Bill 15 would require Texas abortion providers to perform sonograms on all women seeking abortions one to three days before their procedure. It required that sonographers turn the screen so that mothers could see their unborn children and that the sonographer describe aloud the child's physical features. The bill would also require that mothers receive a list of health care providers in the area that would not perform abortions.

I knew that this legislation could empower women with the knowledge they needed to make healthier, more informed choices. It didn't make sense that women were expected to make a choice without the benefit of all the information modern medical technology could easily provide. And I knew, from personal experience, that knowing exactly what was going on in my body could mean the difference between life and death for my child.

My husband, Chris, and I decided that a trip to the Capitol would both give me a chance to tell a story that could influence the life-trajectory of thousands of women in my state and also give my teenage son, Roman, a chance to see the legislative process in action.

Two weeks later, it's the day I'm to testify. The February sky is clear and sunny—a bit warm, but not unusually hot for Texas. I begin strolling with Chris, Roman, and a close friend of mine from our hotel to the Capitol building a few blocks away. I'm wearing a black pencil skirt, white poets blouse, and my red pumps. These shoes remind me that my trust is not in myself but in the One whose blood atonement covers me and offers the strength to follow Him even when I don't feel up to the challenge. Roman matches my colors in his black suit, white shirt, and red tie.

I pray I don't sweat too much.

Once inside the Capitol, we're directed to a large, tan room occupied by a panel of Texas legislators seated in front of a large state seal mounted on the back wall. Facing them is a room full of occupants, many prepared to testify themselves, others waiting to hear the testimony firsthand. Our committee session starts at 1:00 p.m. There are 20 or 30 people waiting to testify. I am scheduled near the end of the session, and it will be more than two hours before my name is called.

Listening to the testimony is excruciating. Some argue that zygotes aren't human; others say that informing women of what is inside their wombs would only humiliate them. I know that we were all once zygotes, and I know that avoiding a discussion of what is growing inside each mother only serves to delay the wave of shame and guilt they might feel after their procedure should they choose to have an abortion.

Dr. Linda Flower, now a dear friend, gets up to speak next.

"Postabortive women often have low birth-weight, pre-term babies," she describes. *That sounds like Roman*, I think to myself. Roman was only four pounds when he was born.

"To summarize," she says a few minutes later, "the reasons to do a sonogram are to get accurate dates, screen for uterine abnormalities, determine viability, determine the number of fetuses present, help rule out a molar pregnancy which can become malignant, help prevent complications, and give a pregnant woman the chance to make an informed decision, just as she would with any other procedure."

After she steps away from the podium, I hear my name called. But just as I begin to stand and start toward the podium, I hear Roman whisper something in my ear.

"Can I walk up with you?"

I couldn't be more thrilled to have him by my side. But knowing teenagers, saying yes might prompt him to change his mind. Still, I can't say no.

"Do what the Lord leads you to do."

A moment later, we're walking up the aisle toward the podium together. The state representatives, almost all men, are seated on the panel before me, and what feels like hundreds of spectators look on from behind me. Two legislators on the right won't make eye contact with me because they don't agree with my position.

I had been intentional with my attire and appearance. I had no idea whether I would come across as composed, intelligent, and logical, or …not. So I wanted to set myself up as best as I could for success. If my testimony was less than perfect, at least I wanted them to see a beautifully tailored, professional woman who was passionate about what she was saying. Either way, God willing, they would listen.

I lock my hands to the wooden podium, and the Holy Spirit fills me with peace. I only have five minutes to speak, and I'm not here to enter the abortion debate. I'm here to tell my story.

CHAPTER TWO

EARLY YEARS AND GOOD TIMES

If an artist sketched a painting of my childhood, it would feature a vibrant, creative, active, adorable, four-year-old Cindy Sisto. She'd be dancing on the top of a Volkswagen Bug on 16th Street in South Philly, as though hundreds of thousands were in a stadium all around her, cheering her on. In truth, I twirled on a nearly empty street, less than a city block long, dead-ending at a bridge.

My father was probably away at work, but if he'd been home, he would have danced with me. My earliest memory of him is watching him snap his fingers and dance to Johnny Mathis on the radio. He loved to sing and dance. In the early years, he was brilliant, always singing, always dancing—alive.

But life had not been easy for Pete Sisto. My grandfather, his dad, had been physically abusive toward his children. When Pete was nine, his father abandoned the family for another woman. Dad never forgave him, refusing even to attend his funeral. After eighth grade, Pete dropped out of school to work full-time at a butcher shop, providing for his alcoholic mother and three sisters. He started drinking and gambling as a means of escape.

When I was a bit older, I realized my dad really was old Italian, smoking a cigar, and saying things with a thick accent: "Hey, you know, Cyn? How ya doin'?" That's how he talked, as if right out of a movie.

He met my mom when they were in high school. I have a picture of them going to her high school prom. He was 18, she was 16. They married two years later. They had three children: Lisa, Cindy, and Petey (Pete Jr.).

I was due on Christmas day, 1966, but I came nearly a month late, a fact that makes all mothers cringe. Mom refused to have the delivery induced. "The apple will fall when it's ripe," she quoted her own mother as saying. She would leave the date of my birth to God.

God knew the reason. I was born on January 22, 1967. Nobody at the time knew that this baby girl's birthday would later coincide with the landmark decision that would be at the heart of her life's calling. On January 22, 1973, the United States Supreme Court ruled in *Roe v. Wade* that abortion is a fundamental right, subjecting all laws that might restrict it to strict scrutiny.

My first memories of my mother come to me as photographic images. She was a young bride from an Italian family, living in a home on a beautiful row with her strapping new husband, laughing at me, her middle child, dancing on the roof of the Volkswagen parked outside. Before my sixth birthday party, I remember her tenderly pinning up my hair while I squealed with delight over my new beautiful purple and white dress.

I was always expressing myself. A quiet moment from me was a shock for her. I remember one time when I was playing on my Aunt Peggy's floor, completely consumed with the toy in my hands. My mother was amazed that I was so quiet and focused and snuck a photo to savor the moment.

A normal day was filled with dancing, Barbies, interviewing on cassette players, making music compilations, and singing at the top of my lungs. I used to wrap myself in my mother's curtain sheers and spin in the backyard for hours, a wispy, ethereal train gliding away at my back.

I dreamed of becoming an actress and a dancer. My vibrancy drove my mother crazy—in a good way. I was active, unafraid, amped up on life, loved to dance, didn't know a stranger. Within my tiny body, I was larger than life.

My parents made for an amazing young couple, in love with each other, with life, and with being Italian. And in love with their three children. They were deeply connected to family, and they worked overtime to make a better way for our family. My father would pull my pigtails, and we got along when I was young; but as I grew older and started wanting more attention, things changed.

In the early '70s when I was six, my dad packed our bags and drove us down from South Philadelphia to take advantage of a sales job opportunity in Houston. He started working with chemists and selling epoxies, grouts, and resins, and did quite well for himself. He always made sure we had new school clothes and shoes every year. When he was a young boy, he relished receiving new shoes from his step-grandmother, Antoinette, and wanted his kids to experience the same delight.

I have vivid memories of my grade school years. In first grade, I remember Miss Baker (whom I adored) teaching us to golf; pageboy haircuts were all the rage in second grade; third grade was about making new friends; in fourth grade, I sang "Bohemian Rhapsody" by Queen in the elementary school talent show a cappella at the top of my lungs; in fifth grade, I remember creating a backyard carnival to raise money for a Jerry Lewis Telethon.

Both of my parents considered themselves Catholic, but only Mom took us kids to church on Sundays. Sometimes she just sat outside the church in the car and read the newspaper. I liked church myself, but even though there was a time when I was teaching the younger kids, I never really connected with the people there.

My grandmother (we called her Nanny) lived with us and took her Catholicism seriously. I used to wake up in the middle of the night screaming, having nightmares, and she would come into my room and give me her ice blue crystal rosary. It was beautiful, and she would put it in my hands and say something to me in Italian, pat my hands, and go back to her bed. I prayed with it clutched in my hands, and in some way it brought me great peace.

As a young girl, in the back of my mind I always knew God and His presence in my life. From the very beginning, God put a desire in my heart for Him. I remember lying in bed at night at the age of 12, under my canopy, feeling the heart of God. I had the same dreams every young girl must have: my heart longed for the love of a prince, whether the prince was a dad, a husband, or a Heavenly Father. I knew, as I suspect every young girl does deep in her spirit, that I was uniquely me and special. And I knew—a deep, tangible knowing—that my Heavenly Father loved me.

If only I had stayed true to that knowledge.

CHAPTER THREE

ON THE BRINK

My grandmother died when I was 12. The sudden loss of her presence in my everyday life left a hole in me—one I didn't know how to fill. Afterward, I started pushing away from my family, my home—everything that had once been so dear to my heart. A little prematurely, I started acting like a rebellious teen, by challenging my parents.

On a Saturday when I was in sixth grade, I got the notion to take my friends, Joe Bob, Sharon, and Kelly for a joyride in my father's four-door Malibu. After all, the keys were there and, with my parents being at a funeral, I went for it. What I didn't anticipate was my father and mother pulling up into the driveway moments before my return. When I pulled up behind them, my father calmly told my friends to go home and then he proceeded to whip me with his belt—buckle included. A couple of dozen whacks left welts on my back and hives all over my body. Doubtless these were all visible when I went to gymnastics, but no one reported such things back then.

I built up resentment toward my dad for the beating incident, and as the animosity in my heart grew, so did my strong-willed behavior.

I started sneaking out of the house periodically. It wasn't what I did once away from the house that drove me, it was the freedom—the walking away from everything the house and its occupants represented— that propelled me.

Coinciding with this, my mom and dad began struggling in their marriage. My dad was a workaholic, selling at IW Industries by day and bartending at a Steak and Ale restaurant at night to cover the expense of braces for my older sister. He had grown up poor himself, and he was determined to do whatever it took to provide well for our family. He was also an alcoholic and a gambling addict—his means of escape, of numbing himself from the pain of life, especially the pain his own family had brought him while growing up. All of these issues, plus the increasing challenges that I presented, formed a huge wedge that drove my parents apart.

As my behavior grew worse, my father started hitting me. He had never been abusive before. Flawed though it was, this was simply his way of trying to tame the wild teen who had veered off the track. A desperate attempt to get everything back under control. It is the oddest thing as a young girl to deeply sense the love of a father, yet to be on the receiving end of his hand or belt. My heart yearned for his love, but what I got was a whole lot of hurt. It was all he knew, really. He had grown up in a family where he had been hurt too.

So, my defenses kicked in, my walls went up, and I just tried to dismiss it all as normal. But it wasn't normal, and deep down I knew it. By the time I was 15, I had convinced myself that I hated my father. Our relationship grew so bad that my friends and I toyed with the idea of cutting the brakes in his car.

When my earthly father stepped out of my life, giving in to the alcohol use and gambling addiction destroying his marriage, my young heart began to seek love, affirmation, and affection wherever I could find it. My neediness combined with my "I'll-do-whatever-I-want" attitude created the perfect storm in my world.

CHAPTER FOUR

TERRIBLE DECISIONS

Between ninth and tenth grade, my parents' crisis came to a head. Mom, Dad, my Aunt Mena, my brother Peter, and I took a family vacation to Las Vegas. Dad kept a fifth of J&B scotch whiskey under his seat and drank at the wheel. Once we hit Vegas, we only saw him if we joined him gambling.

I was the 15-year-old with the fake ID, sitting with Dad at the blackjack table, gambling and winning. I would hop into a round of play, put all my chips in, win some money, and then take a break to buy an oversized stuffed animal before bidding in the next round.

Dad didn't fare so well. I watched him as he gambled away the money that had come from long nights sweating in a white apron. As usual, it stressed Mom out terribly. Looking back, I realize that was the final straw for her, and the beginning of their end.

They separated. They never intended to separate or divorce, of course. They simply found themselves in the middle of circumstances—some self-made, some not—that they didn't know how to deal with. Separating was their temporary solution. They never found their way back to what they once had.

I became a latchkey kid.

Shortly thereafter, I started drinking when Mom wasn't around and using my fake ID to get into clubs. My friend, Johnna, and I started to talk about what sex was like. She had, for whatever reason, lost her virginity to this 19-year-old guy named Trent who lived across the street from her. Naturally, I was curious. I wanted to know what it was about. So Johnna had a brilliant idea.

"Why don't you lose your virginity to Trent?"

Johnna was saying that she really enjoyed the sex. So why not? It would be the same experience that she had had, so we could compare notes.

At that time, I didn't have a lot of supervision. Mom was working, Dad was working. They were separated. On March 1, 1982, a Monday, I went out to dinner with my brother, Peter, and my dad. Dad and Peter went to stay at my Aunt Nancy's for the night. Trent came over to spend the night with me. We were so scared that my dad was going to come home, but he didn't. We stayed awake all night, eventually getting in the Jacuzzi together, and then later, into my bed. As I put it in my diary, we "made love, sex, whatever you call it." We got up around 7:00 a.m., took showers, and left. As he was leaving, Trent said he wanted to get me to where sex wouldn't hurt.

So there was going to be more, I thought. The next day, I wrote in my diary, "It hurt but it was OK. Trent was so great! Who makes better lovers than friends?"

A cascade of thoughts kept rushing through my mind. *Okay, what was that all about? That was not fun. That does not physically feel good. Why was it enjoyable for Johnna and not enjoyable for me? What's wrong with me that I didn't like it more? Did we do it right?* I was very confused.

At school, I had this sense of being exposed. But the truth was, no one knew. I wanted to tell somebody, but I didn't really know how to talk about what happened. The only person I could talk to was Johnna—and she was over the moon about Trent. I wasn't feeling that at all, but Trent would make it all okay. There was going to be more. He was going to "get me where it wouldn't hurt."

The next night, Trent stayed over again. We got home around 10:00

p.m. and went straight to my bedroom. In my diary later, I wrote that we "tried to make love, but I kept messing it up and went to sleep." This sex thing wasn't going so well, and it was my fault.

On Wednesday, I saw Trent again, but he headed out with another friend. I went into hysterics, hyperventilating. My diary later recorded: "Haven't talked to Trent all day. Johnna came over for a while. I want to die."

I wasn't really contemplating suicide. But to my 15-year-old mind, having this older guy—who was making me feel special, and was going to help me become a woman—blow me off, felt like the end of the world.

The next Saturday, I was out with some girl friends. We had all taken some downers and went to a party. Trent was there and was rude to us. And on top of that, Lisa told me that she had slept with Trent, too. I wasn't feeling very special. But if I wasn't going to get attention from Trent, I was going to get it from somebody.

I can't recall where my parents were or what they were doing during this time. I know I was in the middle of turmoil and Mom was in an anxious state. I'd seen the arguments, seen Mom throw Dad's clothes over the balcony, seen Dad move out.

I could look out of my bedroom window, down the driveway, to the townhouse building that was adjacent to ours. I could see Richard's garage. Richard was a young guy with money who owned his own place. I'd see his roommate, Jay, pull up on his cool Harley. Richard and Jay were 24 and 23. Next door to them were Bobby and Tommy, who were a bit older, almost 30. These four grown men, with nice cars and homes of their own, hung out together and partied. To me, it was the perfect picture of freedom, fun, and escape. And that's what it became.

My best friend and I, a couple of underage girls, started hanging out with these four men. I don't remember how we first made their acquaintance. I remember asking Richard if we could borrow his car to go out. He refused, but somehow we all struck up a relationship. I would sneak over to their townhouse, constantly, and we would all party. We would smoke pot and watch Jay shoot up. Richard lay in bed, mostly, high on something.

Jay, always in and out on his motorcycle, was the one I was attracted to. He was an ex-con, it turned out. I didn't care. I would do whatever he told me to do. I would stir up his crack cocaine, insert it into his syringe, wrap his arm with the band, and watch him put the needle into his arm.

I started doing drugs too. I smoked dope, did cocaine, and became a Quaalude freak. I never put a needle in my arm. Somehow, in His grace, God spared me from lifelong diseases and from getting so hooked on drugs I would never be able to stop. I partied—did drugs—on most days before school and on weekends. During ninth grade, I had 89 absences for my first period class at school.

At this stage in my life, I was so out of control that even if my mother had had an inkling of what was going on, I wouldn't have allowed her to stop me. I was getting attention from big, handsome men who had money and nice cars.

And then there was the sex. From all four of them. My girl friend and I would come home late from a club up the road and pop by to see if the older guys were up. We became their objects.

I don't recall the sex being enjoyable. In fact, I can remember thinking at times that it was disgusting and certainly uncomfortable. I had only lost my virginity a few months before, so it's not surprising it wasn't so great.

As awful as all of this may sound to people who hear it now, at the time it gave me a sense of being included. I felt important to these men. Clearly, my girl friend and I weren't. They weren't concerned about who we were or what we were feeling. They weren't thinking about our innocence or the impact all this might have on us. But we weren't mature enough to realize that. We were just willing participants.

To me, it felt like an adult world. I was included in this little adult circle. We were getting attention and free drugs. So saying no to sex didn't seem right. If we were in their world, we had to follow their lead. I was a 15-year-old girl with a 21-year-old's ID, thinking this must be what 21-year-old women do.

I really hate that I became promiscuous. It makes me so sad looking back at this young girl named Cindy who was tough and bright and owned the world, yet was without direction or vision for her life. So she grabbed the freedom of the world around her and got herself into a complete mess.

Unfortunately, that was just the beginning.

CHAPTER FIVE

PREGNANT

Toward the end of the summer before my sophomore year, something gradually dawned on me.

I might be pregnant.

I had missed a couple of periods and was feeling sick at my stomach, and finally I put two and two together. I was petrified. I didn't know who the father was. Jay, most likely, but I couldn't be sure.

The first person to notice was my first period biology teacher. She led me out into the hallway and said, "Oh, I remember what that felt like." She pointed to a garbage can. "Here, throw up in this." I did. Then she handed me some saltine crackers.

In retrospect, I realize the teacher was, in part, responding to my crisis. She acted with genuine kindness. But she could have been such a game-changer. Instead of just directing me to a trash can, she could have directed me toward people who actually could have helped. But she didn't.

I went on my way, and thinking I was pregnant didn't slow me down or in any way alter my behavior. One night, a guy named Paul, a 30-year-old, came by and picked me up at 12:30 a.m. We went to a club, ate beans, also known as Quaaludes, drank, and danced until 4:00 a.m.

On Labor Day, September 6, 1982, I wrote in my journal:

No school, met Francie [a friend]. Got up and went to the mall from 2:30 to 5:30. Got caught shoplifting. Francie was holding it so she got all the blame. I had to drive her car home. Me and her mom went and got her out of jail.

But finally, on September 9, I knew I had to confront the pregnancy. I sat down at our kitchen table and said, "Mom, I might be pregnant."

She had already suspected. She said she'd noticed that I hadn't been using feminine hygiene products for a while. Already suspecting, however, didn't mean she wasn't very upset. Or that she didn't make me feel extremely guilty.

Mom's first impulse was, "We need to get you an abortion." Now, this went against everything she believed. She was a God-fearing, wonderful, sweet mom, and is my Rock of Gibraltar now. But she wanted to protect my tenuous relationship with my father, and she knew he would kill me. If not literally, then almost.

I was sick the next day, so I stayed home from school and took a home pregnancy test. It was positive. Mom scheduled an abortion for the following week, six days away, at a large abortion clinic near downtown Houston. In my journal, I wrote:

Friday, September 10. I get an abortion Thursday at 9:15 a.m. When Jay called at 3:15 a.m., I told him I was pregnant. He was upset because I didn't tell him. I wished I was still a virgin.

Saturday, September 11. I hate myself for ever losing my virginity. Now, I have to murder mine and Jay's baby.

Monday, September 13. Threw up in the shower before school.

Tuesday, September 14. I threw up in first period.

18

Wednesday, September 15. School, didn't get sick, can't eat from 12 a.m. until after my abortion.

Mom borrowed $300 for the abortion. From whom, I didn't know. She wanted us to pay in cash so that Dad would never find out. A friend of hers came to the clinic with us. Mom checked me in under her friend's name, Annette Wallace. The center felt cold, white, and otherworldly. Did anyone care about what Cindy was feeling? The staff didn't seem to notice anything other the fact that I was next in the queue. They put me under.

When I woke up, it was done. I was lying on a gurney beside a seemingly endless array of other women lying on gurneys around the hall. Someone gave me orange juice and crackers, and then my mother and her friend took me to Denny's. It was surreal. *I just killed my child*, I kept thinking to myself.

When Mom and I got home, we realized we didn't have the house key with us and were locked out. So a few hours after an abortion procedure, I climbed up the railing to the balcony to get in through the glass door.

That night, I wrote:

Thursday, September 16. Went and had my kid murdered. They knocked me out with an IV, with Valium? So I didn't feel a thing. Got a blood test, my blood is RH negative. I wanted mine and Jay's baby so bad.

I cried a little. I seemed more upset by the fact that I could have been living with the father.

Two weeks later, I returned to high school. My biology teacher never followed up with me about our interaction. She never asked me how I was doing. Life went on.

What had happened?

I was 15, a typical teen, acting out, looking for love in all the wrong places, with parents who were busy with their own life situations, and I found myself in an unintended pregnancy. I was scared. I was confused. There wasn't anyone to sit down with me and say, "Slow down. Let's talk about what's happening here." I was a predictable, preventable statistic.

My child would be 35 years old now. I can never forget my first baby.

The problem for 15-year-old Cindy is that life didn't just go on. I was much too young to understand it, but I had just pulled a veil of sin over my own body. As my journal showed, I knew the reality of what I had done. But at 15, I was far too immature to process it, and I certainly didn't know the healing that I would later discover God offered. So I did the only thing a 15-year-old could do. I acted out and simply numbed myself. And in the process, my life spiraled down further and further.

I became more promiscuous. I did more drugs and alcohol. I engaged in more at-risk behaviors. And, of course, at-risk behaviors only took me where I'd already been. In my life, I refused to distinguish between right and wrong.

> *September 17 (the day after my abortion). Me and Gary and Lisa May, and Gary's mom at Steak and Ale, sat and drank from 8:00 p.m. until midnight.*
>
> *September 18. Went to the Prickly Pear, drank margaritas. Got home around 2:00 a.m. Brad called and came over from 4 a.m. to 5 a.m. bombed. Dating Paul who is 30.*

Jay would drive his motorcycle over to find me, have his way with me, and drive off into the sunset. I perceived that as love.

My journal indicates the following in December of my sophomore year. I was 15.

- *Skipped school*
- *Had sex with two or three different over-aged guys*
- *Went to visit a probation officer with an older guy friend*
- *Attended the 28th birthday party of one of my four drug guy friends*
- *Did cocaine and Mandrax (a downer)*
- *Spent the night at some guy's house*
- *Went to a club with a 25-year-old; got back home at 8:00 a.m.*

- *Made a cake for CCD (Catholic Sunday school for kids) and taught the CCD class the next day*
- *Went to midnight mass over the Christmas holidays*
- *Broke into a guy's house who didn't have his key; got home at 4:45 a.m.*

That was over a *10-day* period.

Not wanting me to get pregnant again and realizing she couldn't control my behavior, Mom put me on the pill. Around this time, she checked into a mental health center for a nervous breakdown.

Despite it all, God had His hand on me.

CHAPTER SIX

THE PLAN TO SAVE ME

What God used to save me from myself in tenth grade, at least to a degree, were the actions of two coaches. My behavior got their attention, and they devised a plan. They decided to keep me so busy that I wouldn't have time to get into trouble. I was failing their Drivers Ed and history classes. I *had* to pass Drivers Ed, at the least. The coaches said if I wanted to pass, I needed to join the swim team, immediately. Swimming would take up four hours of my school day with intense exercise and leave me exhausted every night. They introduced me to the swim coach and I joined the team. I started swimming from 6 to 8 every morning and 4 to 6 every afternoon.

Their plan succeeded, at least for six months. The swimming completely wore me out. I stopped using drugs. That year was the first I had been drug-free in a long time. I was just too tired to even think about using drugs, or be around people who used drugs.

The swim coach kept me busy with practices, engaged my time with babysitting his three kids, and challenged me to think more highly of myself. He even taught me some practical things, such as showing up to class and taking any extra credit offered to me.

When he found out dancing had always been in my heart, he encouraged me to apply for the High School for the Performing and Visual Arts (HSPVA), a public magnet school in Houston. I auditioned and was accepted in dance. Yet, because of my grades and my questionable behavior record, the school wouldn't enroll me. My coach, though, taught me not to take no for an answer. He had me look at their rationale for turning me away and challenged me to rise to the occasion. I did, raising my grades to straight As before reapplying. I was determined to be a successful dancer, actress, or stage director.

On the outside, everything was looking up. Way up. But on the inside, I was still a wounded child looking for someone to provide the love and attention I couldn't get from my own father. As any young girl in her acting-out state—especially one with a wounded, postabortive heart—I began to look at the swim coach as a sort of savior. To me, although he was only 28, he was a father, a counselor, a psychiatrist, and a guide.

For the first time in my life, an adult had taken an interest in me and begun to see the potential in me. Coach saw through the behavior. He was a well-educated college graduate who recognized my intellect, even though it was colored by my behavior.

He was a very skilled writer who wrote poetry. He began leaving me encouraging notes in my locker. As a young girl, I was able to respond creatively with notes back. It became the only affection and consistent attention I'd had with a person that looked through and beyond the drug-crazed stage. He looked past the promiscuity and saw the potential of the person I could become, and he started speaking to *that* person. At 15, I couldn't articulate that, but I knew that's what was happening:

He sees me, and sees who I really am. He sees I can dance, that I'm an actress, I am skilled at school. I do have potential. I'm not just the horrible kid that gets in trouble all the time, I thought.

I think I started misplacing what his affection was supposed to be, becoming so hungry for it that I turned it into something it shouldn't have been. I was a child with no boundaries and an insatiable appetite for the one person who really saw me. I wanted more.

Six months after I joined the swim team, my coach became my lover. He stayed that way for the next four years. He'd had a vasectomy, so I never got pregnant. I was convinced that I was in love and that we had a future together. From my journal:

> *I'm in love with a [29]-year-old man with a wife and three kids. If she weren't around, things would be fine. We have a seven-year plan. He loves his job, so he doesn't want to jeopardize his work.*

Mixed with the affair were all the other aspirations in my life.

> *I'm practicing for UIL drama after school and I love it. Applications for HSPVA came today. . . . I want to be so close to God. I want to grow in his name.*

Getting close to God was difficult when I was destroying a man's marriage and family.

> *My birthday was beautiful, spent in San Antonio with [my coach].*

The coach's wife found out about the affair after a while, or at least suspected. She would show up at swim meets and confront me. He and I denied being involved with each other. At one of the meets, she and I got into a knockdown fistfight. Needless to say, suspicions were aroused.

> *First spring water polo game. Coach is a nervous wreck. The [main] authority saw us at the Bus Barn and gave coach the third degree. [His wife] lied for us and said it was her. I don't want to lose him back to her. Please know, I finally have no doubts that I absolutely, positively love him. I won't give him away, I won't.*

All this time, I was still trying to make it into the High School for the Performing and Visual Arts.

HSPVA audition, end of April. I love my [coach]. God, I love my [coach]. May the Lord be with us.

Eventually, the full truth came out. He got fired. He and his wife divorced. By that September, he had moved to another state. I traveled to be with him on weekends.

Years later, I had to repent of all the wrong I engaged in concerning this affair. I was underage, yes, but that didn't mean I wasn't making morally wrong choices that had destructive effects in the lives of others. In part, I had to repent to cancel the harvest of this in my own life. I knew that if I sowed adultery and did not repent of it, I would be laying the groundwork for reaping the same if I ever married.

That summer, while our family was in Las Vegas (again), I got the call that I had been accepted into HSPVA. But the school decided that enrolling me was not advisable because I was going into my senior year and it would be too late to switch schools.

During the spring semester of my junior year, I had started attending a Baptist church with Beth, a close friend since elementary school. The pastor would walk up and down the aisle, inviting people to come receive the salvation that Christ offered. I felt that I always knew the Lord, was always drawn to the Lord, and always wanted to be near Him.

I was still sucked into the world, though. My relationship with my coach had kept me off drugs, but it destroyed his life at the time and did great damage to my own heart.

After he was fired, and without my having any healing or stability in the Lord, I floundered. Gradually, I returned to the old fleshly comforts. Promiscuity, drugs, anorexia, bulimia, and all the rest became a regular part of my life once again.

CHAPTER SEVEN

OFF TO COLLEGE

One of the positive things my swim coach did was help me to apply for college and get accepted. I wanted to go someplace as far away from family and as close to his state as I could get while still paying in-state tuition. That landed me at the University of North Texas (then North Texas State), halfway between Dallas and the Oklahoma state line to the north. So, I moved 300 miles away from home to start a new life.

As usual, my heart was in multiple places at once. In my journal, during my first semester at school, I wrote:

> *Thursday, November 14, 1985. I am now a freshman at North Texas State University. I am a drama major. I want to be a college cheerleader. I want to be a recognized actress. I want to be a Christian. I am, but I want to be closer. I want to travel. I want a daughter. I want her name to be Rose. My baby girl, and I'll call her Breezy.*

[That was the nickname my swim coach gave me.] Brown eyes, and sharp as a whip, tiny, all muscle, a little ball of energy. If [coach] is the father, she shall be Christina Rose. Rose, after my Italian grandmother, born October 29, 1901. Rested December 25, 1979. Nanny, I miss you.

Mom and Dad are finally divorced. I have a puppy that [my coach] gave me at graduation, a black cocker spaniel named Dominic Sylvester. Got him in April of 1985. I haven't had sex in five months. [My swim coach] was my last, although he is now seeing someone and has had sex with his new girlfriend. I don't want to curse anymore. I want to rise with Christ and spend eternity with the Lord. I honestly love him. Be with me always, Dear Lord, Jesus Christ. I love you.

In my second semester at North Texas, the book I needed for my English class was inexplicably no longer available. When I mentioned that in class, this guy from across the room raised up his book and said, "I happen to have an extra one. Meet me after class." He didn't really have an extra one. He gave me the book he had purchased for himself as a way to meet me.

His name was Don. He had curly hair, blue eyes, and drove a fun little BMW. The next thing I knew we were pulling over on the highway to his small hometown to have sex on the hood of his Beamer under a full moon.

We dated during my freshman year. We did ecstasy together and drank peach Schnapps, which I liked until I got alcohol poisoning and spent 48 hours vomiting. (I haven't had another peach Schnapps since.) Don's parents owned a lot of land outside a little Texas town—a place I loved—and we used to drive there on weekends.

I went home to Houston for Christmas break, connected with some old high school friends, and did ecstasy with them too. Over spring break, Don and I drove his Beamer to Daytona Beach, Florida, and partied. We returned to Denton and spent lots of time on his waterbed (which I never did like). After the spring term ended, I went back to Houston and discovered I was missing periods.

Enter pregnancy number two. Before Don, I was used to being in a four-year, illicit relationship with a teacher twice my age with whom pregnancy wasn't an issue. With Don, protecting myself from pregnancy wasn't something about which I had given much thought.

I called Don and told him. He sent me money for an abortion. We didn't see each other after that.

Without much thought, I went to see my OB/GYN. She was, at best, five feet one, had mousy-brown hair down to her waist, and had a picture on the wall of her and her eight children. Much later, I learned that she was a leading abortion provider in Houston and that her name was included on a list of abortion doctors with numerous pending malpractice suits.

I was so convinced that my drug use had damaged the pregnancy that having another abortion in her office just seemed like the obvious thing to do. This was, after all, what I had done before, and now that I was pregnant again, I didn't give it much thought.

My doctor certainly did not hesitate to whisk overwhelmed women into the next room and perform D&Cs (dilation and curettage, a common abortion procedure in which the abortionist either sticks a suction tube into the uterus and vacuums the fetus out, or takes a curved instrument and scrapes the lining of the uterus, cutting away the fetus.) That's exactly what she did for my pregnancy. It's astounding to me that I just wandered in so aimlessly and had another abortion.

The date was June 12, 1986. I was 19. The price of terminating a life in me for the second time was $191.

I don't remember much about the pregnancy or the abortion. At the time, I was drugged out, zoned out, and dazed out. For years afterward, I was in denial and told myself that my drug abuse caused bleeding in that pregnancy and that the abortion was just a miscarriage. It was only after God had turned my life around that I faced the fact that I'd had a second abortion at age 19.

Despite what I told myself, I knew what I had done. Now, I had two terminations of life from which I needed to numb myself. This time, instead of running into the arms of a teacher for a four-year affair, I crossed continents.

CHAPTER EIGHT

TO ENGLAND AND BACK

During my freshman year at college, my friend Pippa and I decided it would be fun to be foreign exchange students in England. We applied. We weren't accepted. I don't remember why. Maybe it was all the drugs we listed in the "Experience" section of the application (kidding!).

After my second abortion, we decided to take time off from school and go live in London anyway. Pippa was a lovely creative woman who dreamed big and had big visions. I loved running with her and dreaming big and doing adventurous things. We were there almost six months, working in a pub and drinking cider, and I began sleeping with men left and right. In less than six months, I put more than 40 pounds on my petite, 5'1" frame. While in London (before I had put on all of the 40 pounds), I competed in a world dance competition on the BBC. I also got into a fistfight with some Irish chicks at a tube (subway) station—a knock down drag-out fight. I was scrappy.

We came back to Texas and I reenrolled at North Texas. I decided that I wanted to do something more with my life than party and sleep with guys. I did a personal inventory at the time about my relationship with God. I wrote in my journal:

October 5. *I love [God] and pray for forgiveness. I'm definitely human. God, please don't hate me. I love bubblegum, One Life to Live, Elton John, cheerleading, and Omar. C'est la vie, Breezy. Breezy, I love you. Breezy, I can't wait to know you.*

(It's interesting that I wrote about Breezy as a future child. When I went through postabortion healing years later as an adult, this was the name I gave the child I'd terminated at age 15.)

I started going to church again. I drew nearer to God.

And yet, I couldn't break myself of my all-too-familiar destructive behavior.

Pippa, who at the time was a theater major with me, said, "We're good actors. Why don't we take on the role of a dancers at a strip club and make some money?"

It sounded like a good idea to me. I thought I could play any part I wanted to play. So I took on the role of a topless dancer. Unfortunately, since we were both overweight after our time in London, the only jobs we could get were at pretty skanky clubs in Dallas, where the B-dancers are. I started dancing. And doing drugs, of course. All dancers do drugs. How else is a young woman going to go out on stage and do that night after night?

Dancing brought another idea into my head: I decided to try out for the University of North Texas cheerleading squad. I thought, *I'm an actress. I can play this role too. I can make it believable.*

I'm not sure why I thought I could do it, still carrying my extra 40 pounds. But I had cute short hair at the time, a platinum flattop growing out from my time in London. I put it into a little ponytail, added an extension, and went to the tryout. What was fabulous was that the judges didn't show up, so they had to video our tryouts.

I thought, *I'm a RTV/Film major. I can play to the camera. I don't even have to look at people. They don't have to know I'm not really skilled. I can just act my way through this.*

I convinced myself and had complete confidence. Miraculously, I made the team. I was the overweight cheerleader.

My cheer partner was David Goodrich. He had to throw around the heavy chick. Poor guy. But we actually got to be really good at stunting. When we broke for the summer, I took a summer jogging class. I jogged and jogged and jogged. I hated it, but I thought to myself, *I might not be the most talented cheerleader, and I might not have all the skills, but at least if I run and lose the weight, I'll have endurance. I can at least keep up with everyone.*

Soon I started to run the bleachers at the football stadium. I got addicted to that, and the weight leapt off. When I went back for the fall squad, I was back down to 108 pounds. David and I became the lead stunt couple because I was now the smallest one on the squad.

In addition, I was doing well in school—making good grades. But the positive things in my life were still outweighed by the negatives. Far outweighed.

I was still doing drugs all the time, especially with older guys (again) at a nearby apartment complex. I was a speed fiend. I smoked speed, snorted speed, anything I needed to get it into me.

I was still dancing. Because of my weight loss, I was able to move on to an upscale club in Dallas. Then, I started dancing at private parties (such as bachelor parties)—which, looking back, was just nuts. I'd get an address and I'd go. I would be in the living room with 20 guys surrounding me, and I would dance, and I would make money. Looking back, it was so dangerous. I don't remember having sex at those parties, but I could have been raped by all of them. I just look back and thank God for protecting me.

I was struggling with both anorexia and bulimia. I was sleeping around constantly. As usual, my life was completely out of control. An old day planner entry from December 1, 1987 reads:

> *Make an appointment with Dean. Cheer from three to five. 7:30 basketball game against Baylor, and then work night with Sean [which meant, go strip].*

December 2 reads:

Dance concert. Buy ecstasy.

At that point, my friends and I were doing both ecstasy and speed.

One night while dancing at the club, one of North Texas State's premier football players came in. He knew me, of course, as one of the cheerleaders. He saw me and I saw him. I was horrified. He didn't say anything to me, and I didn't say anything to him, but word got out about it. One night shortly thereafter, I walked out of the club and said, "God, if you'll take care of me, I'll never come back." And I didn't.

CHAPTER NINE

A COMPLETE MESS

What replaced dancing was a whole host of activities that, at the least, were better for me and had a future. I had already started doing some coaching of high school cheerleaders at a nearby gym, in Dallas, and I got more involved with that. I became a photographer at a shop called Flash Photography, primarily shooting fraternity parties. I also became a local news anchor, hosted a movie behind-the-scenes show and a local magazine show, and was the lead instructor for a bad aerobics show. Somehow, in the midst of it all, I took time to study and hold my grades up.

I was like a superwoman, as if I had unnatural power. Because I did.

I had been introduced to Crystal, which was in essence a poor man's cocaine and just a powdered speed. I had also been introduced to people who dealt it. A Crystal dealer would come to my house, chop the drug up, and put it in little baggies. I became a dealer, and speed was the fuel that gave me the ability to keep my grades up. I lived a very busy lifestyle, so speed was my best friend. A little in the morning, a little in the vial in my purse, a little in between classes, a little sniff, a little dap on the tongue, and I kept going. All my friends did it. It gave me a crazy keen focus.

My junior year (on a five-year plan), I decided I wanted to "step." Step dancing was something the African American sororities and fraternities did. They had step shows. I wanted step dancing to be my next thing (as if I didn't have enough things already), so I pledged an African American sorority, Alpha Kappa Alpha. I was "on line" (in a pledge class) for 24 weeks.

And, alas, this provided a whole new population of men to sleep with.

I got beat up during my time on line. Literally. One of my line sisters didn't like me being lead dog (the shortest person on the line, because pledges line up from shortest to tallest). She had me walk on my toes for 24 weeks so another girl would take the lead. I never officially made it into the sorority. Before that time came, the whole organization got kicked off campus, so that was that.

About this time, I was sleeping with a guy who had a girlfriend. One night at 3:00 a.m., she came to my house, sneaked in, and attacked me. The fight was vicious: I put her in a headlock, she bit a chunk out of my arm, and I slammed her into a wall. Someone called the police, and after seeing what we had done to each other, they put both of us in jail. Over time, I would get into a lot of fights.

I had slept around with so many men at this point that the sexually transmitted diseases were piling up. I discovered I had gonorrhea and figured out who gave it to me. I showed up at his house with a gun and shot it into the air, freaking out the two friends who were with me, Denise and Anissa. I cursed him out as he ran to his car and drove off.

The infection got so bad that I lost my vision and couldn't walk. A guy I was dating at the time took me to the doctor—it was my 22nd birthday. When I was checked into the hospital, they found that in addition to state-reportable gonorrhea, I had pelvic inflammation disease (affecting my walking), pre-cervical cancer, genital warts—you name it. I'd probably been exposed to everything and was carrying most of it

The doctor did an emergency laparoscopy for the pelvic inflammation disease. I had to go back for the pre-cervical cancer treatments and had to have all the genital warts burned off. My vision returned fairly quickly. Getting back the movement I lost from the pelvic inflammation disease took longer.

All of these events were piling up so rapidly that I began to reach a breaking point. About this time, I fell in love with a guy named Johnny. We began dating, and things went well until I found out he was also dating a girl from his church. He would be with the church girl, then go do tricks with a prostitute named Claire, and finally turn to me as the little slice of white cake on the side. We broke up once I found all of this out, and I was heartbroken.

I began slipping into a clinical depression. Because I really didn't have a support system, I wasn't sure who to turn to or how to work through these feelings that were overwhelming me. I felt as if I were being sucked into a bottomless pit, and I dropped to 98 pounds.

For the first time in my life, I started to feel the gravity of the tragedy that was my first abortion. The veil of sin was ripped back, if only briefly. I was driving my car when the realization of what an abortion was came to me. I started sobbing, and hyperventilating, and crying, "Oh my God! Oh my God!"

I was at least able to partially mourn the loss of my first child. Because of my drug use, I was still in denial about the second one. I was convinced that it had been a miscarriage, but it wasn't. I have paperwork from the clinic that clearly indicates it was an abortion.

I decided to start seeing a counselor at Pastoral Care in Dallas, who helped me begin to understand why I was pining and grasping for someone's affection. She desperately tried to explain to me that if I invested in myself, believed in myself, and quit trying to latch on to men to fulfill the void in my life, then perhaps even the men I cared for would be more attracted to my self-dignity versus the needy leach I had become.

In my clinical depression, I couldn't quit crying. I cried all the time. I would wake up crying, call my mom to cry, cry on the way to work, and then cry on the way back home. I was finally fired because I couldn't pull it together. My counselor gave me freedom to cry, but in order to help me get the depression under control, she prescribed Prozac and suggested I schedule "cry times." Instead of crying all day in every environment, she told me to give myself a window to cry, and to cry it out. Then she suggested that when this window of time ended, I should pull myself together and focus on the task at hand. It worked. I began scheduling my cry times, and every time I got in my car, my driving time became my cry time. The tears turned on from the time I got in the car and flowed the whole way until I arrived at my destination, where I would force myself to have the strength to turn them off. Over time, the tears subsided.

I went on to graduate with a Bachelor of Applied Arts and Science in Radio, TV, and Film, Applied Behavioral Analysis, and Social Work. I had been a North Texas cheerleader for three years, I had gained some good experience in television, and I was still a cheer coach.

The reality was that my life was a total wreck, but I would come to learn that God specializes in lives that are a complete mess.

CHAPTER TEN

GROWING UP (SORT OF)

S hortly before graduating, I was sitting on a pew in my Catholic church. I remember saying to God, "Okay, God, if you're real, you have to show me. I'll do my part. I'll show up here every week." Looking back, it was a rather immature approach to God, but that's where my heart was. Despite my many wrong choices in the years that followed, it was a kind of spiritual rebirth for me. I began a trajectory on which I was increasingly serious about God and my relationship with Him.

The real work in my heart, in a sense, was God bringing me to the place where I was finally able to look head-on at what my sins really had been. Because there were plenty of times after this when I found myself saying, "I don't want to remember. I don't want to remember my past." I had already been running away and hiding for years. That is what God had to deal with.

After graduation in 1991, I decided to stay in Denton. I was managing Cheerobics, a competitive gym, and I was teaching aerobics. I finally came out of the horrible yearlong depression that had begun right before my graduation.

With Kimberly, my college cheerleading coach, I coached collegiate cheerleading and choreographed routines from 1991 to 1995. We were traveling the globe, coaching, and judging competitions. In 1995, I coached the North Texas State team of 20 cheerleaders to their first national NCAA Division One cheerleading championship.

During this period, I also slipped in working for Reliance Mortgage Company for three years. As usual, I had my hand in more cookie jars than the normal person would ever dream of.

I was still drinking heavily, doing drugs, taking my antidepressants, and having promiscuous sex. Every February, Kimberly and I would take a vacation to Mexico before starting our traveling on the worldwide cheerleading circuit. We were the poster children for "What happens in Mexico, stays in Mexico."

Through it all, I was going to church, and falling more in love with Jesus (seriously). I was on my feet, ministering to my cheerleaders, and growing up a little.

I know it seems odd. How could I be living in both directions? It was a struggle to be sure. Maybe part of me wanted Christ so badly, but another part of me "knew what I was, and couldn't believe that I'd ever fully change."

In 1993, in the middle of all of this, I moved down Interstate 35 from Denton to Dallas. I was waiting tables at Uncle Julio's Restaurant and met this guy, named Travis, who was graduating from SMU. He was an actor, film writer, and producer, and I was now an actress with an agent in Dallas. We started dating, and my journal says that on June 24, 1993, we went to a Steven Curtis Chapman Christian concert in Dallas. The following day, I talked to an attorney about handling a DWI I had been charged with.

That fall, Travis and I got engaged. We were attending St Luke's Methodist Church and went through premarital counseling. We ordered engagement photos and began working with a wedding planner named Teddy. Our wedding was scheduled for June 25, 1994.

But broken people don't do relationships well. I was one of those broken people. It caused strife and endless fights in my relationships.

I had secured a job as spokesperson for Sally Beauty Supply, a role I had for four years; and I did their corporate training videos once a month. Feeling unsure about my relationship for no other reason than that I had never been committed before, I began getting cold feet. I remember doing a shoot for my job a few weeks before the wedding and being a nervous wreck.

During that time, I traveled to and from Houston a lot, visiting family. My family is full-blooded Italian, so my sister and her live-in boyfriend, John, hung out with a group of local Italians in Houston. One of these Italians, Gordon*, was the best friend of my sister's boyfriend. I would come home and stay at my sister's house or stay at my mother's house, so I became the natural choice to be set up with John's best friend. I was the Italian sister in from college. At the family functions and holiday parties, Gordon and I struck up—I wouldn't say a "friendship"— but a connection. I would come to Houston often, and the connection grew until he and I became involved.

Meanwhile, I was still scheduled to get married in June. I think I had broken a crown and had a dental appointment in Dallas. When I went under the laughing gas, my thoughts overwhelmed me. Somehow, I got what I perceived was clarity about my situation, and I realized there was no way I could get married.

I ended the relationship with Travis.

Right on the heels of my breakup, I began to fantasize about Gordon, having an Italian family, and being with someone who understood Italian culture. He drove a BMW and owned his own business, and that all sounded appealing to me: history, legacy, Italian babies, wealth, and security, security, security.

By August, Gordon and I were visiting his hometown together. I moved back to Houston to be with him. At the time, I was straddling two worlds. I was getting more serious about my faith. In my own way, I was loving Jesus. But Gordon and I were still sleeping together, of course. This was the guy I was going to marry (I thought), and no one waited to have sex before marriage anymore, did they? My life was a constant battle between Christ and the world.

---

* Name changed for privacy

I was attending St. Michael Catholic Church every week, and Gordon came with me. I was beginning to realize he wasn't the dream man I had built up in my head. After church, he would light up a joint in the parking lot and then spend the afternoon smoking pot, drinking, and cursing. We fought all the time. He called me a whore and kicked me out of his house. But he didn't stop sleeping with me, of course. And in all fairness, I didn't stop sleeping with him either.

I took a sales job at Thomas Reprographics. Stephen, my boss, became a mentor and helped me get acclimated in the new sales role. He was 30-something, and I was 20-something. We would take our work conversations over to a nearby Mexican food restaurant, and we begin to share our lives with each other. I learned that he was married but feeling unappreciated by his wife. I was dating Gordon but having a horrible experience with him.

So Stephen and I began commiserating over beer, and chips, and salsa. Once again, I was attracted to a man in a position of authority over me. Stephen and I began confiding in one another and finding solace in one another. He was on the outs with his wife, and I was on the outs with Gordon—the whole reason I moved to Houston in the first place. Alcohol helps bring a person's guard down, and one thing leads to another.

By September, Stephen and I were sleeping together. Here I was again. I remember thinking, *this will just be a September fling, and at the end of September we will be done.* But we weren't. I was still having sex with both Stephen and Gordon in October.

In November, I went to the doctor's office for a routine checkup. I was in for a major surprise.

"You're pregnant."

Again.

Here we go, pregnancy number three.

CHAPTER ELEVEN

NUMBER THREE

I panicked. In part, because I was pregnant again. And in part, because I didn't know who the father was. *Gordon is going to kill me, and Stephen is still married.*

I called my brother from the doctor's office, freaking out. "I'm pregnant! I'm pregnant! What am I going to do?"

I'd recently switched to my mother's church, so when I got back home I called there.

"Can I speak with a priest?"

I simply told him I was in a bad spot, facing a terrible problem.

"Whatever you're going through, you're going make the right decision," he told me. In truth, he had no idea of the dilemma that I faced. Our conversation didn't go deep enough. But he kindly sent me a note after our call, which I found genuinely encouraging. That note is still in my keepsake box.

I was 29, growing in my faith, and in a much different place than I had been as a teen. There was certainly not a good rationale as to why an abortion would be my immediate thought. I wasn't married and didn't plan on having a child, but I was at least more mature now, had a good job, and was old enough to know better.

But I had a long-established habit. I had a learned behavior. You abort unintended pregnancies. That fixes the problem. I had already done it twice. That was my conditioned response.

I don't know how long I wrestled over the decision to abort a third time. I remember overhearing a pro-life commentator on the radio one day on the way to work. I actually said to God, "Lord, you'll forgive me just one more time, won't you?"

I began bleeding during the pregnancy—a common issue for postabortive women, although I didn't know that at the time. I had also bled through my pregnancy at age 19. I was around nine or 10 weeks along at this point. I decided to go to see my OB/GYN, who had performed my last D&C in her office.

I showed up still in a state of crisis, crying hysterically to the nurse: "Is it Gordon's? Is it Stephen's?"

I told my doctor the dilemma. I didn't know who the father was. Either the big, fat Italian guy, or the blond guy with blue eyes.

"It'll be pretty obvious who the father is," I said.

"Who do you want the father to be?" she asked.

"Well, the Italian guy, I guess."

"Then tell him it's his baby," she advised. "Dark-haired and dark-eyed people have light-haired, light-eyed babies all the time."

"You mean lie to him?"

The whole thing shocked me. I was already in crisis, and here was this doctor telling me to lie about who the father was, and live with it the rest of my life.

She did a pelvic exam. "Oh, you're bleeding. It's probably a miscarriage."

She knew how distressed I was about both the father and the irregular bleeding. She was trying to comfort me with words that are best described as a guess. There was no way for her to know whether I was miscarrying or not. But instead of giving me the truth, the facts, and my options, she simply jumped to a conclusion.

Here's where my frustration comes in. I was old enough, and had enough personal experience, to know better. I was old enough to know that this was something that should have been tested, instead of simply assumed.

The staff had already drawn for a blood test and found that the hormone levels in my blood stream were very high. They ran the test again. If it were a healthy pregnancy, the levels should have increased. But the second time I took the test, my levels had gone down from 200 to 100. My doctor assumed that confirmed a miscarriage.

What she failed to pay attention to were the abnormally high hCG levels—a strong indicator of multiple pregnancies. She saw my vulnerability. She knew I was lying there on the table, still bleeding, feeling high anxiety and unable to process things well. But rather than discuss the full test results with me, she simply said, "Let's just do a D&C."

They wheeled me from one suite to the next to scrape the baby out of my womb. The doctor performed the abortion without providing anesthesia, and I just about squeezed off the hands of the nurse standing behind me. I was rigid and my stomach was a clenched ball.

The nurse said to me, "Relax."

"I can't relax!"

I was a wreck. My body simply would not cooperate, as if it were fighting to preserve the life inside of it.

After she'd finished the procedure, the doctor put the fetal matter into a jar in my sight. I couldn't make out the body parts, but I could see flesh.

"It looks like we got everything," she said.

So, number three. Three abortions. Ka-ching! I was a repeat customer. Not once, but twice.

I hate being a statistic.

CHAPTER TWELVE

LIFE

After abortion number three, something wasn't right. I had been living at my mother's house in Houston, but my furniture was at the townhouse of Johnna's (my 8th grade best friend) mother, Billie. So I drove up to Dallas to retrieve what I had left there and complete my move. I was carrying my mattress down two flights of stairs and I thought, "I'm exhausted. Why is this wearing me out? I'm strong, I can do this. Why am I so exhausted?"

Two weeks after the abortion, I returned to the clinic for a routine postabortion checkup. The same doctor did a pelvic exam.

"Your uterus is still very enlarged. We probably didn't get everything."

Uh…what? Didn't get everything?

I struggled to process what I'd just heard.

I began freaking out again. "What do you mean?"

She repeated, "We probably didn't get everything out of you the first time. Your body still thinks it's pregnant."

She was ready to wheel me into the next room and perform another D&C. She hadn't ever performed an ultrasound to see what was inside me; it wasn't required by law at the time.

I had just had my third unintended pregnancy, but I was beginning to return to the Lord, and something reacted inside my heart. By the grace of God, my arm went up, and I said, "Can I see what's inside of me?"

She responded, "I can send you to the hospital to get an ultrasound."

At that point, I think she realized what had happened. Instead of performing an ultrasound herself, she simply wanted to get rid of me. She didn't want another lawsuit for a botched abortion.

I went to the hospital to get an ultrasound. The technician was scanning, and scanning, and scanning. She went to get her supervisor and they scanned some more.

"Can you tell me what's going on?" I asked.

Not knowing about my recent abortion, the nurse replied, "The baby is moving so quickly we can't get a steady image."

"Baby? What baby?"

She turned the screen toward me so that I could see. The screen revealed a deflated gestational sac to the right and one intact sac to the left. I was still pregnant with a healthy, 5.3-centimeter fetus, swimming like mad, with a perfectly strong heartbeat.

Realization came fast and furious, and was overwhelming.

You're pregnant. You're not pregnant. You were carrying twins. You lost a twin. You had an abortion, but one twin survived.

I was delirious.

But one thing was clear. This was a miracle. And I knew I could not have another abortion.

Simply by being informed, fully informed, aware of what was going on inside of me, the life of my unborn child was preserved.

I walked out of the hospital, got into the black Infiniti I'd borrowed from my sister, drove out of the parking lot, and wrecked it right down the street. Needless to say, I was in emotional shock and had no business driving a car!

Not long after, I drove by a Catholic church I knew of. They had a Gabriel Project sign out in front that said, "If you're pregnant out of wedlock, we're here for you." I parked and went into the office, in complete distress and at the end of my rope. Inside the church office, the secretary pointed to the sanctuary and said, "You can pray in there." I went to the fifth pew from the back on the left side, knelt down, and bawled my eyes out. But in that moment, the Holy Spirit offered sweet comfort. The Lord spoke to me, saying, "I created life." And a life was still inside me.

CHAPTER THIRTEEN

ROMAN

I couldn't think past the moment I was in. I had to focus on getting through each day, and letting the next day worry about itself. In hindsight, it was an amazing journey. In the moment, it was the most overwhelming thing in the world.

I was on my own. Gordon drifted away. Stephen's wife found out about our affair. She keyed my car, and then I lost my job at Thomas Reprographics. I got a job as an executive assistant to one of the owners at Texas Video and Post, doing film transcriptions, film company disbursements, and whatever. The owner and the company were great to me, a prospective single mom whose head was going in a thousand directions.

My pregnancy was a huge wake-up call for me, spiritually. On my own now, with a baby on the way, I really had no one else to cling to but Christ. It's amazing how God steers our journey, especially during such circumstances, taking our own bad choices and their consequences, and putting them to work for His good in our lives.

For so long I had been straddling the fence between living for what the world offered and living for Christ—mostly the former. With a baby on the way, for the first time in my life, I started to get serious about living in God's will. It wasn't a once-and-for-all commitment. It was simply a daily thing. *God, what do you want me to do today?* My whole life became just day to day.

Other than the occasional bleeding (once again, common for postabortive women), my pregnancy was perfectly normal. Until it wasn't.

On February 29, a second ultrasound showed a healthy, well-developed, and perfectly formed baby. We were 75 percent sure it was a girl, due July 1, 1996. On April 18, a third ultrasound once more showed a healthy, perfectly formed baby . . . boy. There wasn't any doubt this time. He had full round cheeks, lots of hair, and weighed in at 3.5 pounds. The technician said the thigh bone was long, indicating a tall height. I couldn't stop thinking about how precious he was! He was now due on June 29.

On Wednesday, May 8, I completed my last childbirth class. That evening I bought a baby crib. I went to bed and woke up at 2:45 a.m., leaking fluid. There was more fluid an hour later. At 4:00 a.m., I called the hospital. My mom, who just happened to be spending the night with me, checked me into the hospital at 4:45 a.m. with a ruptured membrane. My water had broken seven weeks early. Fearing the baby's lungs were not fully formed, my doctor put me on Brethine to stop contractions and gave the baby cortisone shots to help his lungs strengthen quickly. We waited at the hospital for Mother Nature to kick back in and the delivery to happen. Nothing. My risk of infection had gone down, so on Sunday, May 12, Mother's Day, I was sent home to wait it out.

Except I didn't stay at home. I spent the whole day with my sister at her bridal shoot on the Rice University Campus, working with the photographer. It was an incredibly stupid move on the part of anyone whose water had already broken and who was trying to delay delivery. Again, I was uninformed and failed to ask questions.

On Monday, I woke up with some minor contractions. I walked, breathed, slept, and prayed. At noon I got up to go to the bathroom and something felt funny. I looked down and saw the umbilical cord hanging out. I called Grandma Donna, my stepmother and a nurse, who told me to get down on all fours, bottom up, head down, to keep the pressure off the cord. The fire truck and ambulance arrived within 20 minutes to transport me to Spring Branch Medical Center on the west side of Houston.

The situation was life-threatening for both me and the baby. My physician, Dr. Reiner, and the fireman EMT, Kenny, were on the radio with each other the whole way to the hospital. I had a short dress on with no undergarments and was positioned upside down for all to see. Kenny's fingers were keeping my vaginal wall open, off the prolapsed umbilical cord. He had the cord in his other hand, taking the baby's heart rate as I, my head by the floor, stared at his black Reeboks.

About two blocks from the hospital, Kenny cried out into the radio, "Forty beats per minute! We are losing him!"

Dr. Reiner responded, "Rodeo her," which meant wrapping my wrist tightly so that a vein would pop out. Kenny put a needle in me to knock me out.

What I didn't know, then, was that the baby's heart had stopped by the time we got to the parking lot. He had died.

But Dr. Reiner and the nurse were in the parking lot waiting for us. That may happen routinely on TV dramas, but not as often in real life. They threw me on a gurney and started cutting on me as they wheeled me in. The last thing I saw before I went under was Dr. Reiner's scalpel.

They were able to resuscitate the baby. At 12:50 p.m., on Monday, May 13, 1996, baby boy Sisto arrived. He was 4.9 pounds, and 17.5 inches long. I named him Roman. During my pregnancy, the Lord had impressed upon me Romans 8:28:

> *And we know that God causes all things to work together*
> *for good to those who love God, to those who are called*
> *according to His purpose.*

That's what God had done. He had brought forth a miracle out of my last termination, causing it to work for good.

Like all babies, little Roman lost weight after his birth. As a preemie, he didn't have much weight to lose. He had to fight hard to get a foothold on life, but he passed each test with flying colors. On Tuesday, he got his oxygen tubes taken out. By Thursday, he was doing so well on formula that we tried breastfeeding. He did better than all the big boy babies, latching on immediately and feeding well. By Friday, he was back up to 4.1 pounds and breastfeeding twice a day. His formula intake had increased to 20 CCs, up from five CCs. I wrote in my journal:

> *Baby Roman is still in the hospital under wonderful supervision. Expected homecoming date is first week of June. Mom and Roman say their prayers every night, and little Roman continues to beat the odds. Hang in there Romie, and thank you Jesus for this precious little gift that is certainly a true miracle baby.*

What my journal didn't reflect was the spiritual and emotional struggle I was going through (without being fully aware of what I was going through). Largely because of my abortions, I was genuinely unable to connect intimately with my firstborn son. I had such guilt and low self-esteem and a sense of utter worthlessness because of what I had done. After he was born, when I saw Roman there on the hot plate, with tubes all in him, I thought, *I'm not holding him. He's too small. I'm not holding him.* I have since come to understand that my reaction to Roman is very symptomatic of postabortive women. Other than the brief times we tried to get him to breastfeed, I didn't hold him for a week. My mom and stepmom were the first ones to touch and hold him. To this day, they are his biggest fans.

Despite my own struggles, Roman grew. Two weeks later, he weighed in at 5.4 pounds. I gave him his first bath at the hospital.

I finally brought Roman home, and we settled into life as a little family. My mom became Roman's primary caretaker while I worked. I finally realized I needed to make more money than I was making. There wasn't any room to move up at Texas Video and Post, so I took a job with a competitor, VTTV, at that time the premier postproduction facility in Houston. After a year, I was promoted to general manager, a position for which I would usually have been considered too young. I was managing global production projects—entertainment, music videos, TV commercials, everything—and working there 60 to 80 hours a week. Then I took a second job as the wedding coordinator at my church, St. Michael Catholic, on nights and weekend.

I worked myself ragged, but somehow we managed. I bought a townhouse, and Mom moved in since she was there all the time anyway. God can make something beautiful from anything. Before joining VTTV, I was still a spokesman for Sally Beauty Supply in Dallas. When I drove from Houston to Dallas to do video shoots for Sally Beauty Supply, I would simply load Roman into his baby carrier and take him with me. He would be there during all the shoots, gurgling in his carrier. That October, when Roman was just five months old, I got a letter from Maureen, the executive producer for Sally Beauty.

Dear Cynthia,

You're probably wondering why I'm so absolutely taken with your little Roman. Besides being the most adorable and sweet baby boy, he holds a special place in my heart for a very private reason. Twice in my adult life, I was faced with the same wrenching decision you were, and twice I took a different path. I have no regrets about the way my life has turned out, but I will never fully recover from the choices I made. No child, no man, and no God can ever fill the empty, sad place in my heart that was meant for my two children. It's been a painful and tortured journey at times, but I punished myself for 20 years before I allowed myself to be forgiven.

I will admire and respect you always for your unfailing courage and convictions. I think God and those around you must help you all they can, in every little way, because you are a very special person, a chosen person, and I believe God wanted you to have precious little Roman very badly. Roman will always symbolize for me the faith, hope, and love you have for God, and I know he'll take special care of you always. I want you to know my thoughts and prayers will be with you in your journey with Roman now and always.

All my love,

Maureen

I wrote her back.

Dear Maureen,

Timing is everything. Yesterday was a manic Monday, and my eyes still reflect the stress and frustration of the day. However, just when I think, "Okay, what the hell am I doing? How in the hell did I think I could manage this? Have I done my son an injustice? Am I losing my mind?" and the thoughts are spinning, and my head and my eyes won't turn off, I remember that I have a precious baby boy in my arms. Thank God for small comforts. Just about the time I think I might break, my brother throws a pink envelope across the room. He checks the mail every other day and rarely puts letters in my hand. As I'm holding Roman, I open the card from you and Benny, with a very generous bond, and smile.

My friend, timing is everything, and the kind card, bond, your shared thoughts, and loving support made it all seem okay. I took a deep breath, reminded Roman how much his auntie Maureen loves him, and how special he is to so many people. I thank you for your generosity for Roman. It's strange how the kind gesture of the bond gives a secure thought to this inexperienced mom. My thoughts jumped 18 years down the road, when we might be looking at the bond again for his college plans, and remembering Roman's generous auntie Maureen. As for the private reasons you've shared, oh my friend, what pain. Thank goodness you've allowed yourself to be forgiven. I always picture my lost little ones growing up in heaven in a much better place than I could have ever provided. Yes, I understand the self-forgiveness is the hardest part. I'm sure your babies are safe and sound and at peace with the angels. Perhaps a bit of their spirit is with Roman, giving you and him that special little connection. I just have to keep remembering, one day at a time. You remember, too.

Love and thanks to you and Benny,

Cyn and Roman

CHAPTER FOURTEEN

CHRIS

I argued with God about the next step in my life. A lot. I had been praying for a husband. Roman needed a father, and I sensed that it was time for me to have a life mate. I asked God if He would provide a man who, first, adored Him, second, would truly love Roman, and finally, would love me.

But that makes it all sound way too spiritual. Actually, I was just plain mad at God. I was sitting outside the office building of my employer, VTTV, and I was having a dialogue with Him.

"God," I said, "I don't think I'm *that* ugly, and I don't think you've asked me to live single forever. I would like a tall, dark, handsome, good Christian millionaire who is single, loves you, adores Roman, and then me."

I put out my cigarette and went back inside the building. Then I went back outside with a big P.S. "Oh, and by the way, God, since you made me wait until I was 34 to get married, I would like a ring with a stone that is 3.4 carats. I sighed heavily and shook my finger toward heaven. "Or better!"

The man I actually got was my cycling instructor at the YMCA. He was 29 (four years, four months, and four days younger than me), 149 pounds, pale white (like, glow-in-the-dark alabaster), and, in addition to training cyclists and teaching gymnastics at the Y, he owned a business with his dad.

For Lent, in the spring of 2000, I had given up smoking, dating, shaving, and waxing. In fact, I told God I was through with dating until He showed me the one He wanted for me. I had a gift card from my priest for a three-month membership at the Y. So I quit smoking and started going to the Y. Every time I had an urge to smoke, I went and worked out at the Y, which was within walking distance of my house. Since I was smoking a pack a day, I was at the Y a lot.

That's how I met Chris Wenz.

After we met and started to get to know each other, I knew he was the one God wanted me to marry. Not that I liked it at first.

"God, he's not tall. I wanted someone tall."

"He's taller than you." (That didn't take much; I'm five feet one.)

"He's not dark."

"He used to have dark hair before he started going prematurely gray." I was actually thinking skin tone, but ... okay, God.

"He's . . . he's not that handsome." (I realized later that, due to my own low self-esteem, my perception of "handsome" was greatly skewed.)

"He's my son. That makes him handsome."

"He's not a millionaire. He can't even support me."

"He's the one for you."

"He's not ready for a wife and a four-year-old son and a live-in mother-in-law."

"He's everything you want, just not all at once. He's a good man who loves Me, and you are to love him. Allow him to mature spiritually and financially and love him exactly how he is right now."

Because I was a single mother with limited time, Chris and I "dated" every morning from 4:45 a.m. to 7:00 a.m. He would call to wake me up and then pick me up for spinning (indoor cycling) class by 5:00 a.m. After class, when we were the only two left in the exercise room and had put the extra bikes away, we would have a devotional and prayer time together and then dance until we absolutely had to leave.

Chris wasn't attending church at the time, but there was something about our relationship that reignited his passion for the Lord. We both had a certain "knowing" that God was drawing us together, and Chris became a huge part of my healing journey.

I argued with God for six months about Chris. He just couldn't be the one, could he? I finally asked God one more time, "Is this the man you've chosen for me?" And in my mind's eye, the Lord wrote, mirrored on the inside of my forehead, "YES." I gave in. God had already given Chris a "knowing" about me some time before.

The day Chris met Roman was kind of overwhelming. Roman was four years old at the time. I invited Chris over one afternoon while Roman and I were enjoying a picnic in the grass outside my townhome.

"Mr. Chris" came over and sat with me on the pallet. Around that time, Roman had decided to strip down to play with the water hose. He came running by and jumped in Mr. Chris's lap! It was an awkward introduction, but as Chris would later tell me, and as proved to be true through the years, "Not much freaks me out."

Chris wasn't just a godsend to me, but also to Roman. Roman had been such a game changer for our pre-Chris family. He was the pride and joy of my stepmother, Donna, as well my mother, Rosalie, his full-time caretaker. He was my sidekick who went everywhere with me, to and from Dallas every other week as I traveled for work, on the set of Sally Beauty Supply when I was their spokesperson, and starring in TV commercials when I was a TV producer.

The problem was that he was my little porcelain child. Not that he was fragile by any means, but that's how I treated him. It took a man, Chris, to help Roman mature into a young man instead of a child who always expected to be protected.

We married in June 2001. I married Chris out of obedience to God. Actually, we were married not once but twice.

I had been working as a wedding director at St. Michael Catholic Church, and I dreamed of a wedding on the beach in Mexico. We settled for a traditional church wedding, followed by the beach wedding a week later. We decided to have our initial ceremony in Houston on a Sunday afternoon: Father's Day, June 17, 2001. It went off beautifully—except for the moment Father Steve stood at the front of the audience and recounted all the men I could have had. Why I chose Chris, he said, was beyond him. Yes, he actually said that out loud. Other than that, the wedding went off beautifully!

On Roman's end, he couldn't have been more thrilled to embrace Chris as Daddy. Roman actually did a countdown the week before the wedding. Every day he would ask me, "How many more days until I can call Mr. Chris 'Daddy'?" He had always felt awkward on the sports fields when the kids would ask him who his father was and he didn't have one. As soon as the priest had married us, Roman could no longer contain himself. He ran to Chris and exclaimed "Daddy!"

My prayer was always that God would be a father to Roman while he was fatherless until God chose the one I would marry, and I believe that's exactly what happened. Roman wholeheartedly fell in love with Chris as his Daddy. God couldn't have more terrifically answered my prayer that Roman have a dad who loved him.

The Wednesday after our Houston wedding, we boarded a plane with family and friends and flew to Cancun, where my best friend had done all the planning for a beautiful beach wedding, including having my custom wedding dress made in Mexico. On Sunday, June 24, we had our second wedding. Our spiritual mentor and friend, Rishini Lubanski, traveled with us and married us in an Ephesians 5 covenant of a committed, one and forever, Christ-focused marriage.

For Roman's sake, we decided not to transition our family's living arrangements too quickly after the marriage. Before Chris, it had been me, my mother, and Roman there. When Chris came along, we all mutually agreed that after the wedding Rosalie would continue living with us for six months before she moved out. At his young age, we didn't want Roman thinking that Chris had forced his grandmother out.

Chris and I had our first fight when, after he had treated me with nothing but loving kindness, I got mad and shoved him, just like Elaine did to everyone in *Seinfeld*.

"Why are you being so nice to me?" I screamed. I felt so unworthy and undeserving.

Chris replied calmly that his commitment to me had nothing to do with my behavior and had everything to do with his commitment to our covenant and to Christ. He would have to give an account of his actions to God, he explained.

Honestly, I think God felt sorry for me. He knew where I was heading and the healing that needed to be done, so He simply chipped off a piece of Himself and tossed it down in the form of Chris. Chris was the embodiment of the love of Christ that I so desperately needed. As I mentioned before, from childhood I always knew, deep down, that God loved me deeply. Now He had brought me someone who adored me as He did. God showed His love for me both in the husband He gave me, and also in the process of healing that I was just beginning.

I soon learned to trust Chris fully and began calling him my "Rock Solid Man of God." (That is his name in my phone to this day.) He modeled his covenant commitment to me flawlessly, and that gave me the freedom to heal and rise up to become the woman that God intended me to be. Little did we know that it would take eight years to put the pieces of this broken woman back together.

CHAPTER FIFTEEN

"YOU NEED HELP"

G od had told me to marry Chris, and often at first I simply had to lean upon my knowing that, regardless of whether it seemed to be going well or not. But God knew what He was doing in putting us together. I spent the first part of our marriage going through my healing journey, and Chris was a large part of that healing.

What we discovered through marriage, friendship, and a sincere love for one another was a bond that allowed God to begin peeling back the layers of the healing I needed. It was as if God had sent a piece of Himself in Chris, an ambassador who brought God's message to me when I was unable to hear it from God directly. From Chris, it never felt harsh or pressured; it felt like love and an opportunity to heal. He was a cushion so that I would have the strength to face the many layers that needed to be addressed, parts of my past I had shoved out of my consciousness for so long.

I fondly call this the artichoke season of my healing—God graciously peeling back, layer by layer, only what I could handle at that moment, with the ultimate goal of making my heart right towards Him.

The first eight years of our marriage, Chris was married to a very broken woman still journeying through the healing of multiple abortions and poor relationship choices. In a real sense, we actually began our union in the ninth year of marriage. Before that time, I just had too much healing that I needed to go through.

I had been in survival mode for so many years, including life as a single mother, that it felt extremely weird being someone's wife. I'll never forget the moment I realized I was married, working, loving God, and didn't have to cry out in distress and use my crutch phrase, "I'm a single mother, please help." It was a strange dynamic, slowly stepping into health and wellness.

Chris could tell that I was still broken. He saw my inability to connect from years of distrust and abuse as well as my inability to clear my mind of haunting images and memories from previous relationships. In addition, the soul ties of some other relationships in my life had not yet been cleared out.

My need for healing came out in many ways. I would argue with Chris unnecessarily. I would be defensive. He would ask me about my past and I would shut down.

"I don't want to remember my past! I don't want to remember it!"

My brokenness especially surfaced when I had to go see my OB/GYN. For years I was afraid to go to my doctor. The trauma of all my previous OB/GYN experiences were so etched into my mind that I couldn't get past those painful memories.

One day, at church, I spoke with a prayer warrior who told me that if I had accepted Christ, He had healed me and I could forget about my past. But I couldn't. I knew who I was in Christ by now, but I had not genuinely repented of my abortions and all the other sins of my past. I was still broken on the inside.

We postabortive women often numb ourselves and let the pain lie dormant. One statistic indicates that it takes postabortive women about 10 years to truly recognize the finality of what she did. (We are seeing that time frame shrinking now.) That timeframe is actually a gift, because once recognition comes, the woman can begin to process the abortion. But for me, the pain lay dormant for a very long time. Now, because of Chris, it was coming to the surface. The pain was so great, and the healing so needed.

As my postabortion stress symptoms kept increasing, Chris finally said to me, "Cynthia, you need to get some help. All of this is tearing you up."

But I wasn't ready to go ask for help. I just wanted it all to go away. I asked God to simply take it all away.

At the time, Chris was still teaching a spinning (cycling) class. I did the class with him, and some other couples in the class noticed how we seemed to be growing in our faith walk with God. One of the wives suggested that Chris and I visit Care Net Pregnancy Center of Houston, a pregnancy resource center where she served as a board member. She explained that the center provided support to women in unintended pregnancies, and she thought we might like to be involved. We went to the center and took a tour.

Some time afterward, Chris slipped in a suggestion. "How about that place we toured? Why don't you go volunteer? Maybe if you go and give your healing away, your joy will be made complete."

His words stuck with me. Something about them just seemed right, like God was speaking through my husband. His advice was like the aroma of a divine healing balm. I had no choice but to move forward in faith.

With my husband's words still on my mind, I visited the center with the intention of volunteering. I didn't intend to receive postabortive counseling right away, and I did not yet fully comprehend how much counseling I really needed. But the very wise 24-year-old director said, "Well, if you're gonna volunteer and help with the support of women, you need to go through postabortion recovery. That way you can understand what the many women we serve are going through."

I immediately threw up a front. I didn't want anyone to see how hurt I was.

"Oh, sure, I'd be happy to do that so I can help," I replied smugly. "No problem."

So I entered postabortion recovery with this prayer in mind: *Okay, Lord. You're equipping me, and I'm going to do the best I can.*

I had no idea what I was in for.

CHAPTER SIXTEEN

THE BOYS

Back at the Wenz townhouse, changes came to our family—changes which God used to continue my process of healing.

Chris wasn't able to officially adopt Roman right away. Even an amenable adoption, in which all the parties are in agreement, costs money, which was simply not in our budget. When Roman was in sixth grade, we prioritized the expenditure. An attorney from our church processed the paperwork for Roman's legal adoption, making Chris his official Daddy.

Of course, Roman's biological father, Stephen (yes, I figured out who the father was), had to participate in the process. Roman had previously met him three times. The first time was when Roman was four months old, and the second was a few years after that. Then, when Roman was eight, we visited Stephen's place of employment. So processing the adoption was the fourth time. Roman had always appreciated meeting him and noticed similarities in their appearance, and the way they walked, but his heart was always settled that Chris was his daddy.

I was so appreciative that Stephen cooperated with the adoption process. Roman and I sat down at Escalante's Restaurant, to review the paperwork with him. Stephen had to relinquish all rights to Roman, of course, but he was entirely willing. He knew that God had provided another Daddy for Roman. I had told Roman many times that I had prayed that God would bring just the right father for him, and He had answered that prayer in Chris.

By the time Chris adopted Roman, it was no longer just the three of us. We talked about kids before our marriage, of course, and we wanted to be open to what God has in store for us. We were married in June and conceived our first baby together in December—much earlier than we had anticipated!

I freaked out again. The truth was that I was conditioned toward abortion, not a planned pregnancy. One Sunday morning, shortly after I discovered I was pregnant, I rushed down to the altar at our church, sobbing my eyes out as if I were still a distressed woman in an unintended pregnancy.

"Oh my gosh!" I cried to Pastor Ed, the church's elderly spiritual father. "How are we going to do this? How are we going to do this?"

He responded gently and kindly. "Well, honey, are you married?"

"Yes, sir."

"Is one of you working?"

"Yes, sir."

"Do y'all have a good marriage?"

"Yes, sir."

"Then honey, you are going to be just fine."

He was so kind to pray over me and understand me, simply and lovingly pointing out the obvious. I had to realize that freaking out and pregnancy don't go together. Stressed out and overwhelmed and a new life in the womb don't go together. I had to grow secure in knowing that the life inside me was a child that we were having together.

During the pregnancy, I had a lot of bleeding again. I told my new OB/GYN I wanted the most boring delivery on the face of the planet and that's what he was able to give me. Some research shows that postabortive women, on average, have more preterm deliveries and low-birth-weight babies, both of which were true for me.

Our baby was born a year to the day after the 9/11 attacks. I prayed and felt inspired that I would find his name in the Apostle Paul's letter to the Romans. I kept flipping through the pages looking for a name, when I felt the Holy Spirit in me say, "Actually read." So I read. I got to Romans 8:30 and I immediately knew his name. Paul talks about believers in Christ being justified before God. The name was Justice.

Justice was part of what unified the Chris-Cynthia-Roman unit. Now there was a little brother for all of us to dote on.

Our next son was born two years later. God gave us the name from Numbers 13:30: *And Caleb stilled the people before Moses, and said, "Let us go up at once, and possess it; for we are well able to overcome it."* And Caleb, our son, is as bold, unique, fearless, and faithful as the Caleb of Scripture.

I was 36 when Justice was born and 38 when Caleb came. I had both via C-section, and both at my 38th week instead of carrying to full-term. I had the same bleeding with Caleb that I'd had with Justice, but God kindly allowed both sons to be born perfectly healthy.

The fact that Roman had a different biological father than Justice and Caleb has never been much of an issue. A family of 5 has 25 unique individual relationships to manage, which has always been a bigger issue! God uses unique sitations like these to shape, mature, and create selfless and caring people. It's also the dynamic that can drive a mother and father crazy. But once parents endure the hardest part of it all, the personalities come out stronger, especially when eyes are lifted to Christ and the management of these relationships is in the love of God.

As Roman grew up, there was one issue I agonized over. How in the world was I going to ever tell Roman that I had aborted his twin? Or anything else about my past—that I was sexually active outside of marriage, that I did drugs, that I, that I. . . . Telling him about his twin, though, was the biggest hurdle. I was in angst about it for years. And it was all about me.

As it turned out, God simply bypassed me.

One morning, I was on the phone counseling a friend who had just miscarried, and I was sharing with her "Glory Baby," a Watermark song by Christy Nockles about her miscarriage. I told her how the words touched my own heart when I lost Roman's twin. I was just ministering the love of Christ to her. What I didn't know was that Roman, my preteen, was in the next room, listening to the whole thing. When I hung up the phone, he walked straight in. I froze. And he sat down next to me and asked, "Mom, did I have a sister or brother?"

I didn't have to provide a lot of information. I just straightforwardly answered his questions.

"Yes," I replied.

"Did you abort me? Were you with someone before Daddy?"

It now was becoming his journey, and he was processing. So I answered simply. He wasn't looking for a lot of details. "Yes. Yes. Yes." It was that simple.

And we concluded with this: "Roman, you're the best gift God has ever given me, and you're a miracle."

"Okay, Mom."

And that was that. Later, when I was on staff at the pregnancy resource center, I often thought, "Wow, God. How could I possibly have had this career without Roman knowing?"

God had honored Roman's name. He had worked it all together for good. He always does.

CHAPTER SEVENTEEN

HEALING

I was 41 when I started the 10-week postabortion recovery program. Roman was 12. I went into it with the best of intentions. I wanted to help. I wanted to be equipped. I wanted to represent my church well. After all, I was married to the worship leader at our church.

And I was blind concerning what was really about to happen.

I went through the first five weeks of the program and everything went fine. I was learning. I was being trained. I was figuring out what all those other postabortive women would need to know and do to come to terms with their past.

In week six, I broke. God said, "This isn't about others. This is for you."

For only the second time since the clinical depression black hole in my college years, I realized what abortion was, and that I was responsible for the very dismemberment of the children who once were growing inside my womb. There was a child from when I was 15 who should have been here with us. A child at 19 who should have been with us. There was a second Roman, his twin, who was missing. I was finally able to stop pointing fingers at others. At last, I took responsibility for my own sin and repented of what I had done. For the first time, I could honestly admit, *But by my hands, God.*

There were tears. And tears. And tears. God was healing me.

It was the first time that I was able to mourn the loss of all of my children, who would be ages 35, 31, and 21 today. Even now, I sense their absence. The memory of my children remains ever-present. A mother's heart never forgets.

During the first postabortion recovery program, I focused on the loss of my first child. Then, at the program facilitator's suggestion, I went through the recovery again, focusing on my second child, and then my third. Each child is unique and worthy of intimate attention, and I needed to memorialize each loss and symbolically lay each baby to rest. I was able, in a small way, to give them a measure of the respect they deserved. Each time, I was able to reconcile their loss. Each time, there were more layers that God peeled back, and there was more healing to experience.

At long last, after experiencing the healing of postabortion recovery, the birth of my sons Justice and Caleb, and settling into married life with my Rock Solid Man of God—eight years into my marriage to Chris—I was finally in a place where I could talk about my life without becoming a broken mess on the floor.

God's healing manifested in many different ways, big and small. Here was one. For years after my abortions, I was afraid to visit the doctor's office. The trauma of my past visits, especially to the OB/GYN, had etched painful memories into my mind in such a way that I was afraid to go back. But God healed that.

There was more healing to come, at various times. At this point, though, I had come a very long way down the road.

In the Prologue, I noted that through my choices I became the banner of all statistics. Bad statistics. Abortions. Sexually transmitted diseases. Endless broken relationships.

Early in the process of my healing, I heard God say clearly to me, "I am going to make you My banner now. I will showcase My healing in you. You will be a banner for all to see My redeeming love."

And so He has. To Him be the glory.

CHAPTER EIGHTEEN

CEO

Before going through postabortion recovery and serving clients, I volunteered at Care Net Pregnancy Center of Houston (later to become The Source for Women), doing event planning and coordination. They offered me a part-time position as administrative assistant to the executive director, and I became the organization's bookkeeper at the end of 2008. In June, 2009, the interim CEO left the organization.

That's when God was about to have a good chuckle over me, because they turned around and offered me the job.

I was so angry at God for being offered the CEO position. America was in a deep recession, revenue at The Source was way down, and they couldn't pay me. I don't mean they couldn't offer me a competitive salary. I mean they couldn't pay me at all. Chris was in a commission-based field, and his commissions were down to zero.

I knelt down on a Thursday afternoon and said to God, "Now? Really? You want me to go run this organization?"

And He answered, "For such a time as this."

Planning events, managing a budget, all the activities I had in my life were for such a time as this, to run this nonprofit. And they couldn't pay me. I went home to Chris and ranted. We had three kids with private schools to pay for, and I blurted out, "Would God really call me now to work unpaid as the CEO of a nonprofit?"

Chris just sat in his chair and let me rant. And finally he said, "That's exactly when He would call you."

He's such a man of God.

And I knelt down and said, "Yes, Lord." And then I added, "But feed my children."

I accepted the job, and God continued feeding my children. He did, and He blessed the organization, and it was wonderful. I was able to settle some of The Source's existing debt, then make it debt-free, build up a reserve fund, and finally start to get paid myself. We saw God work miraculously with the young women who walked through our doors. And I saw Him continue to work in my own life as well.

I personally went back through our postabortion recovery program a fourth time as CEO, to audit it. But there was more in it for me.

One night, the class facilitator had us use a dry erase marker to write words that used to describe us on a mirror—words that were no longer true. Then she had us erase them one by one, as God had. It was the first time I could actually look in the mirror at the subtle wrinkles of age and not be repelled at what I saw. I recalled the time in my early 30s, before Chris, when I was dating a guy who, believe it or not, I never slept with. He came to my office at VTTV one day to pick me up and kindly made a comment that I was beautiful. I melted down in front of the project cubbyholes for digi-beta tapes, crying hysterically and scolding him for saying that to me. So for me, looking in a mirror and not hating what I saw was a big deal.

God continued to heal me at an ever-deeper level. I was starting to think, "Yes, Lord, okay, maybe this is going to turn out all right." I was starting to feel, if not on top of the world, then at least a decent way up the mountain.

Then 10 months after I became CEO, in May, 2010, Goliath moved into our backyard. Ten miles down the road, Planned Parenthood opened the largest late-term abortion facility in the Western Hemisphere (the second largest in the world). And all of a sudden I shrunk back down. I felt like Gideon in the Bible. Who was I to fight against such a powerful enemy?

It was as if God came to me and, just as He did with Gideon in the Bible, said, "Oh valiant warrior!" Gideon responded, "Who? Me? A warrior? Valiant? Are you talking to me?" I felt exactly that way. "Goliath is 10 miles from this office, Lord. You want me to be a warrior now? Really?"

The answer was yes.

That plunged me into six months of crying out, "Lord, I don't know how to do this! I don't know how to fight a 100-year-old organization, with government funding, 10 miles from our office, who are aborting all the way until the day before delivery. We're just a small nonprofit! We have one little center."

At 4:45 one morning, I was journaling, and crying, and saying to God, "I don't want this job! Give it to someone else!"

But the word that God gave me that morning was clear: "Do what they do, and do it better, with a message of Life*, and Christ."

I didn't know how we were going to accomplish this mission from the Lord. But I knew that the abortion industry was providing some services to women that actually were needed. Not that they were the only source for such services, but they were providing them. Women actually do need yearly well-woman exams and access to STD testing and treatment. Underserved women actually do need cost-effective reproductive health care. These are the kinds of services that Planned Parenthood and others provide in the front of the house. Then they escort women to the back where they perform the abortions.

But the front yard services are sensible and beneficial. In a way, they were to serve as a model for the health care services I knew we needed to provide the women at our centers with. But I came to realize that we could do it better, in a much more holistic manner that addressed the full range of women's needs. And, of course, when it came to providing

---

* I like to capitalize the "L" in Life because it reminds everyone that true Life is only found in Christ Himself, who said, "I am the Way, and the Truth and the Life."

abortion, the very procedure that robbed me of three of my children, I knew that God was calling us to take a different path.

I don't think I was fully aware of what God was birthing at that time, but this was the start of our holistic model of care: reproductive health centers that are life-affirming, provide preventive medical care, and offer services to support a woman's body, mind, and spirit. We went from being a pregnancy resource center with a volunteer nurse and volunteer Good Samaritan peer counselors—a wonderful foundation—to being medically equipped, holistic reproductive health centers with nurse practitioners, licensed professional counselors, and spiritual mentors to address the full range of women's needs.

God birthed in my heart a "raised standard of care." Women want to know that they're physically well, and they want to know what's happening inside their bodies. Our medical professionals provided for those needs.

Our licensed professional counselors addressed the multitude of life stressors that women who walk through the door are facing. Those life stressors almost always have answers, but women in crisis need someone to come alongside them, identify the good answers, and choose to embrace them. The abortion industry offers women a quick fix. Get rid of this fetus, they say, and all will be well. But all isn't well afterward. The price to be paid is far too high. There are better answers, answers that become apparent to women in crisis when someone sits down with them and invests in their lives.

I loved how one of the directors of the abortion facility was quoted as saying one day, "We are not a counseling center." And I thought, "Well, we are. We are, and we can address the life stressors that are causing these young women to think abortion is their only option."

Finally, our spiritual mentors helped women address their deepest inner needs, seeing who they are as women made in the image of a God who loves them, praying with them, being their advocate, and following up with them.

For the women who needed assistance, we provided that as well. Clothes. Food. Toys. Baby needs. For the women who needed referrals, we assisted them with referrals. We didn't just hand them a piece of paper. We would make the calls for them. We would book the appointments for them. We would make sure they had transportation to go get a second opinion. We wanted to provide for their needs tangibly and *on every level.*

In this way, women who walked through the doors were surrounded by people who cared about their unique circumstance and served them, all in a physical environment that was warm and welcoming and reassuring. Have you ever been in an abortion facility? The place is cold. It's stark. Sometimes it isn't even *clean.* We wanted to be just the opposite, a place that was warm, inviting, with soothing music, scented candles, comforting food, warm decorations, and pristine rooms. We wanted everything about the environment, and our staff, to shout, "You are wanted here! You are valued here! You are seen, and heard, and honored here!"

I believe we achieved that. It wasn't easy, and it wasn't cheap. Love never is. But it's worth it.

So how does this model capture the market share of the abortion providers? Simple. We take their clients, and we take their revenue. We offer a better product. In my tenure at The Source for Women, we *did* offer a better product. We weren't about being *against* something. We were about being *for* something. We were for educated, equipped, empowered women whose full range of needs were being addressed.

As a practical matter, what was necessary to take the abortion providers' revenue stream? How do they make their billions? Through Medicaid. In Texas, they also get their revenue through the state Women's Health Program. We researched the Women's Health Program to learn what we needed to do to be eligible. Then we made sure we had everything we needed, and we became eligible for Texas Women's Health Program funding. We looked at Medicaid. What would it take to be eligible? Would it jeopardize our core values and our core belief in who we were? Absolutely not. We became the first Medicaid-providing, holistic reproductive healthcare center, with life-affirming Christ-centeredness.

Take their market share. Expand in Texas. Take it to the nation. Go global. Welcome Christ's return! That was the vision. It still is my vision.

Could this actually happen? For hundreds of years, there was another industry that brought death, not life, to millions. All the money was on its side. All the politicians were on its side. All the power was on its side. It was the transatlantic slave trade.

The only thing the other side had to offer was truth. But they won.

We have truth, life, love, and genuine care for the needs of women on our side. It's a winning combination. And one more thing. We have a big God. Those who defeated the slave trade were praying believers who had a big God. He hasn't changed.

CHAPTER NINETEEN

EMPOWERMENT

This book is about the story of God's healing in my life. It's not a primer on how to run a holistic reproductive health center. However, the two topics do overlap. Part of the reason I needed such healing was that I didn't have anyone in my life at age 15 to be a first responder. I didn't have anyone who knew how to lovingly address the issues in my life. In addition, learning how to be a first responder in other women's lives has been a big part of the process that God has used to bring full healing to my own life. As Chris said to me long ago, "Your joy will be made complete when you give it away."

I would like to share some of the things I've learned about being a first responder. As I do, I'd like you to keep in mind that we can—and so many of us must—be a first responder in the lives of the young women around us. It's by no means simply a job for people at pregnancy resource centers. In fact, the more of us lovingly intervening in the lives of young women in our own homes, our extended families, our schools, our churches, and our youth programs, the better off our whole society will be.

What I have learned must be our heart as first responders, caring for a generation that grew up with legalized abortion. You will have to tailor this to your own situation, but so many of the principles apply wherever you serve. In the cause for Life, we are all first responders, a trusted friend that someone confides in during a trying time in their life. That may be a young woman discovering an unintended pregnancy, or any life-changing moment which, when shared, makes the one receiving the news a first responder.

Certainly, we want to be the first responder when a teen is in crisis. We want to be there to build that relationship with her. If, as a 15-year-old, I'd had a first responder there for me, my first abortion could have been intercepted. That would have prevented numbers two and three. The cycle can be broken.

But a first responder doesn't have to wait for a crisis. We want to be there before the crisis hits, before the unintended pregnancy.

Information is key. Kids are so smart these days. In counseling, they don't care, at least at first, that I love them, or that abortion is wrong, that it's dismembering a child. They just want the facts. "Give me the statistics. Give me medical truths that don't lie. Tell me what's happening with my body. Tell me what an abortion really is."

So we educate. We inform. We embrace. We equip.

Teens can make decisions when they know the facts, and they know the options. They really can. We speak their language. We speak it briefly, efficiently, and effectively. And they respond.

One in four sexually active teens will contract a sexually transmitted disease. Roman, who's now 21, said to me one day, "Mom, can you imagine if I meet the girl God brings to me. Then what do I do?"

Say, "Well, I made some choices as a teen and now I'm one of those one in four, and now I've gotta just share some information with you about a disease I contracted because I didn't wait." Like I said, the stats register with teens.

We may make use of programs that are abstinence-based and Christ-centered, but those are not words that 15-year-old girls relate to. If I say to a girl, "Please be abstinent. Jesus loves you," she's just going to tune out. It's not necessarily that she's consciously chosen to reject that message. It just doesn't mean anything to her. Teens are numb to the message of abstinence. For most of them, it doesn't speak to the specific world that they live in.

So we have to respect that. We have to respect that, in so many of these girls' lives, their worlds have already collapsed around them. Their family has broken apart. There are two dads, maybe a couple of moms, mixed siblings who compete for attention. They may be victims of abuse. Very often, they experience addiction in their immediate family. They feel vulnerable. They *are* vulnerable. No wonder the allure of sex and alcohol and drugs, and sending illicit messages, is so strong. They are seeking escape. They are seeking meaning. They are seeking love.

So we say to such a girl, "Slow down. Take a deep breath." And we, as the community of Christ, help empower them. "What kind of relationships do you want? What does a healthy relationship even look like?" And they don't know, because healthy relationships have never been modeled to them. So we help them define that, until it seeps down into their hearts.

We talk about lifestyle with them. "How does your lifestyle—the way you are living now—how will that affect the relationship that you want, that your heart longs for?" Then we help them establish goals. We set a future vision that they can embrace, because it comes from them.

It has to come from them. It has to all be done in their language, at their level. They are worthy of that dignity, that respect, that honor. This is educating and equipping and empowering them. Otherwise, it's just lecturing them. And we all know how kids can tune out lectures!

Sometimes parents need to be helped with their perspective, too. In the early years, a mother said to me, "She's sexually active. She's going to be sexually active. I just want to bring her in for birth control and get the HPV vaccine. At least she'll be safe." I find that perspective sad. I didn't have the maturity to respond in the most effective manner at the time, but now I would say to her, "Maybe you're assuming something that doesn't have to be true. What if we were to start by providing some birth control education, so your daughter knows what she's getting into, and what she'll be protected from and what she won't be protected from—not just disease, I mean, but emotional and relational repercussions as well."

Loving parents would want their daughter to be informed first—to be educated, equipped, and empowered to make good life choices. It helps to have a third party who is willing to say, "Is it really in your best interest to go down that path? Let's slow down and get educated." Most young women aren't going to say, "I don't want to be educated. I don't want to be empowered. I'd rather be a victim. I'd rather be a statistic." Who has that as a life goal?

If a girl is pregnant, education is still vital, perhaps even more so. If we show a young woman real medical truth on an ultrasound machine—if we refrain from our own opinions and just let the technology educate her, she will take in what it's saying. She will digest it herself. She will see the baby. She will ask appropriate questions. Wisdom will rise up. Informed choices can be made.

When talking with young women, I have found that content creation is the key. They have been programmed by advertising and a thousand media messages to think a certain way about sexuality and reproduction. Unfortunately, it's a very distorted view of reality. We have to reframe the message for them in a way that makes sense to them.

We have to change hearts. Changing laws is vital—it's why I was at the Texas State Capitol testifying—but the greatest change has to take place through changed hearts

My background is advertising. I realize that a change of heart starts with the messaging that is presented to a young woman. What was the content that had been placed in front of me by the time I was 15? "Everybody gets an abortion. It's a simple procedure. It's no big deal. You'll barely know it happened. Your life can go on like normal. You can have as many children as you want later. Just do it; it's legal."

That was the messaging, the advertising message, that I bought into. That's what we have to redefine.

So we rephrase some very basic truths. We don't say, "You have three choices in a pregnancy situation." We say, "You have two life choices. You can parent your child or you can choose (again: choice, empowerment) to make an adoption plan. Planning takes time and courage. Those are your two life choices. Or you can terminate your pregnancy. So you have two life choices or a termination of pregnancy." That in and of itself is educational.

With my background in TV and producing commercials, I sometimes visualize things as if they are a television commercial. Imagine this: a 13-year-old girl, darling, gorgeous, probably a little, well, physically mature. She's talking with a girlfriend standing next to her, twirling her hair, chewing gum. A very cute boy who is 16 and has a car comes up and says, "Hey, you wanna drive to the lake?" What young, blossoming girl doesn't want to be recognized by a hot teenager? Let's imagine that she turns to him, smiles, and says, "Okay, listen. I'm gonna be the president of the United States someday, so the decisions I make now are important. Going to the lake would put me in a situation where I might have to make some choices I'm not ready to make. So, you're welcome to call me, and we can FaceTime each other, but that's it."

That's called empowerment. The girl has been able to form some lifestyle boundaries that empower her to say *no* to things, to delay gratification, to pursue future goals and objectives with wisdom and love because she's been equipped to do so.

Maya (not her real name) was a girl having unprotected sex under the influence of alcohol and drugs. She was afraid she might have caught an STD. When she came through our doors, we tested her for STDs. A staff nurse practitioner educated her about STD symptoms and prevention. A licensed professional counselor talked to her about making good life decisions. A spiritual mentor talked and prayed with her. In Maya's own words:

> *I confess I was uneasy going to The Source at first. What if they judged me? But as soon as I arrived, my first impression was comfort. In fact, I questioned if I was at the right place. . . . Not once did they pressure me. I felt like they really cared about me and my concerns. I realized that I didn't think anyone really cared about those things anymore. They showed me something I had not seen in a while. They showed me the love of God.*

> *Because of the care I received, I am changed for the better in so many ways. I've stopped doing drugs, and have even stopped smoking cigarettes as well. I took a step*

toward getting a better job, and am now insured and working full-time! This August, I will be going back to school. I plan to be a forensic nurse and continue to share the love and encouragement offered to me.

During my time at The Source, we saw these kinds of results all the time—young women being empowered. I envision an entire generation of young women who have been empowered this way.

CHAPTER TWENTY

BEING FOR

I was watching a video clip recently of a question-and-answer period after a speaker's presentation. A pro-choice young woman got up and asked, "Why do you think it's not about women's bodies and just about a separate life? Like, after the baby is born, how come more people don't care about them? They don't care about whether they end up in foster care, they don't care about the mother being poor."

The speaker didn't agree that was his position at all. And sometimes I feel like asking such questioners, "Rather than just assuming people don't care, have you looked into what organizations in your community are caring for women in these situations?" Usually, they are just uninformed.

But there is a deeper point to the question which always needs to be faced. It is this: we must be known by what we are for, not what we are against. We are *for* women. We are *for* women being educated. We are *for* them being empowered. We are *for* their needs being met. We have a Savior who is so much *for* them that He went to a cross and died for them.

The time when the rubber really meets the road on this issue is this: what happens when we provide a young woman with all the education, emotional support, and spiritual support she needs, but she still chooses to terminate her pregnancy even after she sees the baby inside her is alive and healthy?

That's hard. The Bible tells us that we can have a lot of things— in this case, all the right educational programs, all the right medical equipment, all the trained medical and licensed counselor personnel— but without love we have nothing. The first thing that a woman in that situation needs is unconditional love and support. We are not God. It's not our place to judge her. If she makes such a decision, I know this: the life circumstances surrounding her feel more overwhelming to her than the decision she just made. Thank God for Christ's redemptive grace. It's the reason I can look forward to seeing my first three children in heaven. I can look forward to that, instead of wallowing in guilt and self-condemnation. And, truthfully, we are all in that same boat, regardless of what our sins have been. Because of Christ, we can look forward to a future that we don't deserve.

What is very hopeful in the here-and-now is that sometimes that choice by a young woman is fertile ground for God's breakthrough in her life. She wasn't ready to fully hear when she made that decision. But when she is in the aftermath of it, we know, statistically, that several things will happen. Most likely, she will act out sexually and wind up in the same place again. Except that the next time, she will have the experience of having someone she trusts, who has loved her and treated her with respect and dignity, regardless of the choices she made. She won't forget that.

We educate, we equip, we support, and we love. The young woman may say, "I don't think I need counseling." We say, "Okay, fine. I am here for you." We plant the seed of love. It's going to be *her* journey. We leave open doors that can be a part of her healing journey when she's ready.

That's hard sometimes. We pour so much into women and then if they decide to terminate the pregnancy, it's easy to think, "What else could I have done? I should have done something else." It's easy to feel personally responsible for someone else's decision.

I'll never forget a client who was 10 weeks pregnant and chose to terminate. She said, "This baby's gonna be my guardian angel." I—the key word is "I"—felt like a complete failure. I named her baby "baby August," after the month she terminated. I celebrated his 10 weeks *in utero*, and I mourned. And I still remember, years later.

What I had to realize is that it's not about me. When I talk to a woman, I have a testimony, and I also have a Savior. But I'm not her savior. And it takes spiritual maturity to recognize that even in the termination decision, God is at work. Not that He makes that decision, of course, but He is bigger than our decisions, and His plan is not thwarted.

So many times, my staff and I would get mad at God. "You knew she was gonna do that, God! Why'd you let her do it?" Granted, it hurts. It's not what we expect when we work with our clients, and it hurts. It's never an easy journey.

But God is not deaf, or dumb, or blind. He is not unaware. How dare we would think He'd turn a blind eye. We die to ourselves and resurrect to the omniscient, magnificent power of the Savior we call Lord.

I think that when we ask, "What could I have done," God is purging us. He is maturing us so we can be more effective and more dependent on Him as He moves us out of our way, so that He Himself can move.

My greatest experience of this concerned my own healing journey. I finally got angry at God and said to Him, "You used me. You knew I would abort. I was your pawn. And I'm furious at You for it." And all He breathed into my spirit was, "I never left you. I never forsook you. I was there, weeping with you. And I have your precious ones with me." He reminded me,

> You didn't know, Cynthia, but I did. I knew. You thought you named Roman as you did because he survived the womb. I named him Roman because I knew I would work a far greater good for you, for Roman, and for countless others. I knew you would be my CEO for my holistic care model. I knew you would be my Joan of Arc for women and their unborn children. I know what's down that timeline of life.

And I know you've gone through hell to get here, but you're going to do it with your whole heart, because you've experienced my grace. And we've only just begun. The miracle has only just started.

I have to worship a God who could take my sins and bring something beautiful out of them like that.

Sometimes a woman just isn't ready for what we have to offer. I don't mean the medical services. I mean the counseling and spiritual care. Or the postabortion recovery. A woman may say, "You know, I had an abortion, and I've heard about postabortion stress, but it hasn't affected me at all. I'm fine with it."

We have to honor that. I would never tell a woman what she should be feeling, or experiencing. Studies show that, on average, it takes about 10 years for a woman to recognize and face that an abortion actually took the life of a child from the womb. I know in my heart she will one day have a "come to Jesus" moment. It will wake her up in the middle of the night and she will recognize what happened in the past, and what her choice actually was.

In the present, I would lovingly say to her, "Why isn't it something you can talk about?" Biblically, we know that anything that's in the dark will be brought into the light. That can be pretty daunting. I have three children in heaven. Had someone told me, "Your entire life's calling will involve confessing your sin, not of one, or two, but three abortions. That's going to be everything you talk about for the rest of your life." That's not something you want to hear. So I would simply say to a woman, "Consider what's being left in the dark." I would let that seed marinate and see what God does with it. When you are healed from something, it's because you brought it out into the light. You've allowed God to deal with it in you. If someone's not ready for that yet, they're not ready. The Lord was so kind to me and brought my healing on in layers when I was able to handle it, and He is not a respecter of persons.

As I said earlier, without love we are nothing. What we ultimately have to offer women is the love and life of Jesus Christ. We do care about the choices they make. But even more than that, we care about *them*. We share our very lives with them.

As the Apostle Paul wrote:

> Having so fond an affection for you, we were well-pleased
> to impart to you not only the gospel of God but also our
> own lives, because you had become very dear to us.
>
> *1 Thessalonians 2:8*

I had the opportunity to speak at Baylor College of Medicine. Afterward, I got an email from the Pro-Life Club president there, which beautifully sums up the difference between having an agenda and loving. She wrote:

> *Cynthia, thank you so much for what you placed before us today. We have been reluctant to call ourselves Pro-Life, because Pro-Life, as we know it and as we see it, is not really pro-life. It's antiabortion. And to be Pro-Choice isn't really pro-choice, because they don't support that a woman can make a choice. It's really proabortion. But what you have given us today is a vision that truly supports women—for women, by women, with women, to give them something they can be for, holistically, with preventive care, with aftercare, and something to move forward productively.*

She got it. That young woman saw the problem, and she saw the solution. And she can actively be part of the solution.

The bottom line is this: as the community of Christ, we are for women. That's not hard to be, because we serve a God who is more for women than, in this life, any of us will fully be able to understand.

CHAPTER TWENTY-ONE

AT THE CAPITOL: PART 2

"**M**y name is Cynthia Sisto Wenz. When I was 15, my mother rushed me into an abortion. I aborted again at 19. At 29, I should have known better. I went to the same doctor I did at 19. I should have known better, but I was still unwed. I was bleeding, and the doctor said, 'Oh, you must be miscarrying ...'"

How do you tell about the taking of three innocent lives in five minutes? If you were me, standing in front of the representatives inside the Texas State Capitol, several things helped.

First was Roman standing next to me, lending not just emotional support, but being the very heart of what I was there to say.

Second was knowing that my history wasn't really my story anymore. It was His story. I love that. I simply say, "Yes, Lord, I will be obedient. I will tell my story, which is really Your story." A big part of His story is that I have three children whom I have not yet met, but whom I will meet someday in heaven.

Third was my "Blood of Jesus" pumps. I didn't want to go to the Capitol. In fact, a few days after I got the invitation, I found myself sitting on the floor in my closet, crying my eyes out about it. God knew I didn't want to go. So as I sat there weeping, I looked over at my five-inch red pumps that were sitting there, and I sensed God saying to me, "Walk on the blood." I realized what He was saying: the pumps were blood red—the Blood of Jesus. I had been healed for life by the blood of the Lamb. Now on that blood I would symbolically stand—healed for the life that I took from the womb, healed for my own life that God redeemed, healed for each life in heaven that I now longed to see. Now, I would also be "heeled" in stature to feel tall in the Lord, seen, and heard in such a way as to add impact to the story I was going to tell the state legislators.

I still wear my pumps when I speak at events. When I walk onto a stage or up to a podium, they remind me that I am walking on the blood of Jesus, the blood that was shed on the cross to cover all of my sins. *All* of my sins. I can stand and speak as a woman fully forgiven, fully redeemed, fully healed by her Lord.

As I stood at the podium, the Holy Spirit filled me with peace. I continued.

"Two weeks after my third abortion, I went back to the doctor for a checkup, not feeling well. My uterus was still enlarged. 'We probably didn't get everything the first time,' my doctor said. She wanted to do another D&C. Another abortion. Despite my highly agitated state, I simply raised my hand. 'Can I please see what we didn't get?'

"She sent me to a nearby hospital for an ultrasound. The technician was having a hard time getting a good image. She called her supervisor in. 'Can you tell me what's going on?' I asked. The supervisor replied, 'The baby is swimming so fast that we can't get a steady image.'

"I said, 'Baby?! What baby?'"

I could tell my story hit home. The representatives were paying very close attention.

"I had been pregnant with twins. The abortion had only removed one of them. The other one survived. It was swimming, fast."

I turned briefly and looked at Roman.

"Gentlemen, that thing we didn't get is my son, Roman. His DNA doesn't match any of the DNA of the children I previously aborted, or the other children I currently parent. He is a unique human being. And he is still swimming. He just made the junior varsity swim team at his high school."

Roman put his arm around me and hugged me. The room erupted in applause. The chairman of the committee rose, pointed his finger at Roman, and in a booming voice said, "Son, that's the best thing that I've seen all day!"

I gathered myself and spoke on. "Flash forward. I have a husband and a pregnancy. I am bleeding through my pregnancy. But my second son, Justice, is born unharmed, perfect in every way. My third child is now born. I bled through that pregnancy too. Bleeding during pregnancy, especially for a postabortive woman, is not necessarily a sign of miscarriage. Had I been given the chance to see what was going on inside my body with medical technology that is available, I could have made an informed choice. I would not have had to look at the doctor in my crisis and deferred to her expertise.

"I am now the CEO of a Pregnancy Resource Center for such a time as this. And there is not a woman who will come into that facility and leave uneducated when technology is available. We have a 4-D ultrasound, and there is no charge, no prejudice, and nothing I expect her to do. She has a right to see what is inside her.

"Educate, educate, educate. Why are walking around blindfolded when education is now available? It is her choice, it was my choice. Why wasn't I better educated? Why didn't I get to see until after I aborted Roman's twin, that there could have been two of him? Why couldn't I have full disclosure to make an informed choice? Didn't I have a right to be given all the relevant information, not just the selected information the abortion industry chose to provide? If it was truly my choice, I had a right to have *all* the information."

After testifying for six and a half minutes, I breathed a sigh of relief. Roman and I walked back to where Chris was sitting. We had done it.

Two things happened as a result of that hearing. The bill passed the Texas House of Representatives, and then the Texas Senate, and became law. As a result, Texas abortion providers must now perform sonograms one to three days before an abortion procedure, and let the mother see it. They must also provide women with a list of local health care providers who do not perform abortions.

Something else happened too. I think that day Roman became a man. He pulled his shoulders back and put his arm around me and we stood there together before the Texas House. And the law passed. I think at that point it settled in Roman's heart who he is, and the story that God has him to tell. After that, slowly, but surely, he started to tell his story. A while later, he got in the car after church one Sunday and said, "Mom, they were taking about Romans 8:28 and I shared my story." He's taking more and more opportunities to share his story.

When I named Roman, I thought Romans 8:28 was about him surviving my womb. And it certainly was that. But it was more. I never dreamed that I would be at the Texas State Capitol, helping thousands of women gain access to the information they would need to make informed choices. Once again, God truly had worked all things together for good.

CHAPTER TWENTY-TWO

THROUGH ROMAN'S EYES

by Roman Wenz

I remember sitting outside my mother's room when I was 12 years old, listening to her talk with a friend of hers who had recently had a miscarriage. She shared her testimony with, prayed for, and comforted this woman, telling her that she, too, had gone through a very hard time. As I listened to her speak, I mulled over the words she was saying: abortion, prolapsed cord, emergency C-section—all these things that she was saying were things I had heard before but never understood. Listening to her that night was the first time I began to understand what really happened during her pregnancy with me. As soon as she hung up the phone, I walked into her room and asked, "Mom, did you want me?" I remember her looking at me with tears in her eyes and saying, "Of course I did, Roman. You're the greatest gift God has ever given me." That was the only answer I ever needed.

As I grew older I understood more and more of the testimony we share. The first thing a lot of people ask me when they hear my story is "How do you feel about your mother?" To me this is the easiest question they could ever ask. I love my mother and she loves me. The only time I doubted how she felt about me was the moment I asked her if she wanted me. She answered and I was satisfied. Throughout my whole life, I've carried my testimony. And only in recent years have I understood how great it truly is. When I was younger, all I could think about was how cool it is, and how cool people would think I was when they heard it. But as I grow older I realize how powerful it is, and how God can use it to reach people's hearts.

I remember the day I went to the Texas House of Representatives with my mother as she spoke in front of them. I remember walking up with her, and, though I didn't say a word, I knew God was using me. I didn't need to speak, my mother did that, but I was the tangible, visible evidence of God's miraculous power for everyone in that room. I know God has a plan in store for me, and I know my testimony is a part of that.

To be honest, sometimes it feels like a burden. I love my parents so much, but I feel a lot of pressure due to my testimony. Every time it's shared and I'm in the room, people always come up to me and tell me how big of a calling God has on my life, or the amazing things God is going to use me for. I've always felt like people have been speaking incredible things over me that I will never live up to. But what I've come to realize as I've gotten older is that, whatever I do in my life, as long as I'm following the Lord, it will be for His glory. I will serve Him well, and He will use me. I just have to follow Him. I don't have to be the guy who ends abortion, or becomes the leader of the nation's largest pro-life group. I just need to follow God and use the incredible testimony He has given me to show His glory.

I've seen God's love reflected in both my mom and my dad. For the first four years of my life, I didn't have a dad. I had an incredible single mother and grandparents and other family members who surrounded me and did everything to take care of me. My mom sacrificed so much and worked so hard to give me everything I could ever want or need. And she never stopped doing that, either. Now, I've been blessed to go to a wonderful private college. I've never needed anything more than what she has provided. When I was young, though, I did want a dad. All of my friends had one and I just had an incredible mom. But when my dad came into my life and my parents got married, I was so happy.

This past summer I interned in New York City, in Manhattan. I became good friends with a few of the other interns. One night, while having a long conversation with one of my close friends, he asked me, "How do you feel about your biological father? If you got a call tomorrow and were told he had passed away, would you feel like you had missed out on getting to know him?" That question was like a baseball placed on the tee for me, so I hit it out of the park without hesitation. I immediately told him no. As soon as my parents were married, my dad was Chris Wenz. Any void I had for a father, or desire for a father connection, was filled immediately by him. And the most incredible thing about it to me is that he chose me. I'm not trying to say that my bond with my father is better than the bond my brothers have with him, or any other person's with their biological father. But their fathers had sex with their mothers and they were created, not specifically chosen.

To me, my relationship with my father is extremely special. My dad had to choose me. He met my mother, who was 34 years old with a 4-year-old son, and he decided that he wanted to be a part of our lives. The decision to date and then marry my mom wasn't just about his relationship with her. It was also about his relationship with me. We came together in one package and he chose to take us both. And not only that, but he is the best father I could have ever imagined, and the best husband to my mother. He loves us unconditionally, and both of them have worked extremely hard to provide care for my brothers and me. The way that my father and my mother love me is a direct reflection of Christ's love for all of us. And if their love is only a fraction of his, I can't even begin to fathom how much God loves me.

My parents are incredible, and God has blessed us with an incredible story. I've been with my mother sometimes when she's preparing to give her testimony and she's discouraged, saying, "Why did all of this happened to me? Why did God give me the story? Why couldn't my life have been different?" I always say to her, "Mom, God gave you this story to reach other people. He gave you the story so that He could use it and work through you to help other people that are in your situation, or just even facing a hard time. The story that God has given you, however difficult it may be, is something that He can use to reach anyone He wants to."

I love my parents, I love my mom, and I know they both love me. God has given us our story and I know He has a plan for me to share it. I have no anger against my mother, or a burden that I feel by being who I am. I see a call on my life and I am ready to follow God's plan for me.

CHAPTER TWENTY-THREE

LOOKING BACK—AND FORWARD

I am a healed woman of God. I am a woman healed by God. I'm no longer a broken woman, crying uncontrollable tears over my lost children. God has done a miracle in my life.

I believe I am a small catalyst in the mixture of God's antidote to abortion. He has taken me through seemingly every experience known to women, in the most dire of circumstances, to prepare me to serve women like those I meet every day. I've been through it all: the broken family, the abuse, the three abortions, the promiscuity, the drugs, the loss of vision from ophthalmic migraines induced by birth control, the heart stress and heart murmurs, the pelvic inflammatory disease, the case of gonorrhea, the cervical pre-cancer, the genital warts, the relational dysfunction and pain—these are the crises that the women who come for help face. I've walked this road. And a sovereign God has chosen to use that to bring life to other women in crises and to their unborn children. I just have to marvel at what He can do.

The truth is, after a life of drugs and having contracted nearly every STD around, I shouldn't even be here. I shouldn't have made it to 50. But God brought me through it all. He healed me of every STD. I am disease-free. How kind has God been to me? In my life, the extremity of my sin displays the power of God's redemption even more vividly. As the Apostle Paul wrote, "Where sin abounded, grace abounded all the more."

Once, during an interview, Marvin Olasky of *World Magazine* asked me, "Do you envision the children you lost in heaven? What would you say to them?"

"I do," I answered. "I see them."

I envision my 35-year-old, my 31-year-old, and my 21-year-old in heaven. I've prayed, asking the Lord to show me if they are boys or girls. I have a picture in my brain that they're darling girls. I can see the oldest one: she's got long, brown, wavy hair. The middle one has wispy, not-so-great hair like her Mom's. And the youngest one is a gorgeous female version of Roman. This is my mommy's heart.

I arrive in heaven beside them, and I have a moment of no words, just embraces. And that's it. I always envision them from the back. And I see that long beautiful hair. I see them hanging out with my dad, who has already been there for 13 years now—even though the first abortion was meant to prevent him from knowing his teenage daughter had conceived out of wedlock, he's the lucky one who got to meet my children first.

What God can redeem knows no limits. I mentioned my dad and the abuse I suffered from him. He didn't want to be abusive. It's just all he knew, because of his own family of origin. He could get really mad and lash out in the only way he knew how. But God worked mightily in his life. Although he was a "cultural Catholic," he never went to church much and certainly never understood his need to place his faith personally in Jesus Christ and His death and resurrection. My son Roman had the incredible privilege of sharing that truth with him and seeing God use him to help lead my own father to Christ. He went to be with the Lord 13 years ago. I can't wait to see him again.

Roman's life has been so redeemed. As you can imagine, a story like Roman's is pretty overwhelming for a young man to hold in the back of his mind. For the longest time, he felt a lot of pressure. He thought he had to become an attorney and take a case to the Supreme Court and be the one to overturn *Roe v. Wade.* He doesn't feel that kind of pressure anymore. He knows that all he has to be is who God made him to be. Nothing more. Nothing less.

Roman's 21 now and I'll ask him, "Can you let me hold you?" I didn't hold him the first week of his life. He helps me make up for that first week by letting me just hug those big broad shoulders of his.

Not long ago, I had the opportunity to speak at a fundraising event in New Jersey and Roman and his girlfriend (now wife) drove up for it from their college in Virginia. I told my story, and when it came to reveal Roman's miraculous survival, I asked him to stand in the crowd.

At that moment, I felt a weighty sense of the incredible peace of God. I leaned on the podium, looking through the bright lights shining around me, to look my son in the face.

"Roman, you're a miracle simply because you're here," I said. "46,000 have died in New Jersey over the last year through abortion, but you are one of the survivors. Every one of these people here in this audience are survivors; you are not alone." Surviving the womb is a "thing" now to be celebrated, who would have ever thought?

Whatever your role in the abortion saga in this country, you are not alone. Each of us has been affected by abortion in some way. Whether we're the mother who terminated, the boyfriend who pressured her to do it, or the boyfriend who felt helpless at a choice told to him. The teen who didn't realize the consequences, the friend who paid for an abortion, or someone else—each of us has experienced a graduating class that was smaller than it would have been, the silence of laughter that would have been enjoyed, or the hurt of a missing sibling. Each of us has been affected, and each of us now has a part to play in others' redemption and in the redemption of our nation.

But playing that role usually means being intentional. That's a choice we have to make. I mentioned earlier that after I got pregnant the third time, I drove by St. Michael Catholic Church. They had a Gabriel Project sign out in front that indicated their desire to help with unintended pregnancies. But when I went inside, the lady at the desk didn't acknowledge my distress at all. She didn't honor what the sign out front said. She basically just pointed to the sanctuary and said, "You can pray in there." *She wasn't being intentional.*

Chris and I got engaged at that church, we married there, and Roman and Justice were baptized there. I was hired as the part-time wedding coordinator there and handled over a thousand weddings at that church. Whenever I walked past it, I always remembered the pew there where I bawled my eyes out and God spoke to me.

Fast forward a number of years to when I was CEO of The Source. A Catholic woman was teaching our postabortion healing class, and she brought in the woman who runs all such programs for the local Catholic diocese. I told the woman my story of having gone to the church when I was in distress. I said, "Let's rectify that problem at all of your parishes around the city. Let's make the people at your front desks true first responders." She replied, "That's a great idea. Let's do it."

She *was* being intentional. She wanted all the front desk people in her diocese to be first responders. And they did it. They trained them. The opportunity had always been there. It simply took someone to be intentional about doing it.

What if there had been someone who had been intentional with me?

My story is not uncommon. I was a kid from a family whose life took a wrong turn. Several of them. I wanted love. I started sleeping around. I started drinking. I did drugs. As a minor, I took life from my own womb and was too immature to be able to process it. So, very predictably, my wayward behavior increased. I tried to numb myself. I was simply a kid who went haywire.

The whole time there was this parallel story of a girl who knew God, who wanted to walk with Christ, who had a heart for Him. That's evident in my journal entries. But the world was pulling me away from Him, and I chose to go right along with that pull.

My coaches did try to intervene, occupying my time with the swim team. My swim coach pulled me out of a very destructive drug scene in high school, which saved my life. But then it went too far, ending with a grown man being in a relationship with a minor. That kind of sin, left unconfessed and unreconciled, was even more destructive for our souls.

Tragically, my story borders on the *norm*. Not in its extremes, of course. But because one in three women by age 45 in this country have had an abortion. *One in three!* Where were the first responders for those tens of millions of women? Were there people in their lives who saw the destructive path they were on but were unwilling to respond, not just once, but as many times as necessary? It only takes changing one life to break the cycle for the next generation.

Unfortunately for our nation, we don't hear the voices of those one in three who have had an abortion. That huge group of women have not yet taken a stand to say, "This was wrong." If they did, it would be like Mothers against Drunk Driving. When mothers had finally had enough of the thousands of alcohol-induced accidents in which our children were getting killed and maimed, Mothers against Drunk Driving rose up. We saw heightened awareness and a willingness to discuss the issues. As a result, the drunk driving rate decreased. Mothers against Drunk Driving made drivers wiser.

Can we care enough about the hearts of God's children to speak up? Can we care enough about our culture to be willing to share our story? Can we care enough about being who we are in the body of Christ?

We live in a culture that desperately needs our voice. Our culture tells us, "It's OK. That promiscuous lifestyle is OK. And abortion is your choice. It's your right. Go ahead and end that life." But if Jesus says, "I am the way, and the truth, and the life," and life was extracted from the womb, then in reality we have crushed the very thing Christ says He is. How then do you reconcile a child that was extracted and dismembered from a mother's womb without Christ? I think the bottom line answer is you don't. The only way a mother can truly reconcile the dismemberment of her own child at her own hands is through the redeeming blood of Jesus Christ. My prayer is that God will use my story to open women's hearts to Him, that they may turn to Him, put their trust in Christ, and find the healing that only He can give.

Then once we, as women, have experienced the healing and redemption that only Christ offers us, why wouldn't our voice—that of healed and redeemed women—be one calling out to this generation? If there were a multitude of those voices in our nation, could they not make wise choices in sexual activity cool?

I want every woman to tell a story that says:

> Hey, America, we are speaking up. We can know more, so our children and our culture and our generation can say *no more* to sexual immorality that does nothing but hurt our children, hurt our hearts, hurt our physical well-being, hurt the way we think and feel about ourselves. We can disrupt the downward spiral of sexual promiscuity, sexual freedom, and the way we even think about sex. We can disrupt that and create a culture where morality is the new rebellion.

I want to close by extending an invitation. It is this: I invite you to tell your story. Whatever it may be, tell your story. Jesus said to His disciples,

> You are the light of the world. A city set on a hill cannot be hidden; nor does anyone light a lamp and put in under a basket, but on the lampstand, and it gives light to all who are in the house.
> *Matthew 5:14–15*

For too long we have hidden our stories. We have hidden our light, who is actually Christ. Revelation 12:11 says of believers, "And they overcame him because of the blood of the Lamb and because of the word of their testimony, and they did not love their life even when faced with death."

Others need to hear the word of our testimony. Let's let our stories out. Let's bring them into the light. Let's let others see the redemption that God has worked in our lives, and is working in our lives. We are Christ's body. We are His hands and feet. Others need to feel His touch. They need to hear His story that is our story.

They need to know that He can redeem, and He can heal.

If you are still in need of your own healing or just need your voice heard, I want to listen. Call me directly at 713-385-4169. Your voice matters, and I would love to begin the conversation with you.

With all my heart,

Cynthia Wenz

ACKNOWLEDGMENTS

When I was thinking about how to make my 50th year a significant milestone, I considered many exciting possibilities: pursuing an accounting degree or a master's in social work, training for a marathon, piercing my nose, dying my hair like a holy Cruella De Vil, getting a tattoo, or becoming an author.

So what did I do? I dyed my hair holy Cruella (a quickly fixed mistake), and watched my life transfer from memories and penned journal pages to the chapters of a book.

As I look back at how it all came together, the divinity of each uniquely appointed person along the way that has made this journey possible is astounding.

When Jeff Lane helped me write my first public testimony in third person seven years ago, he crafted it in such a way that I could divulge the hard, painful moments of the story with empathy for the young girl that I spoke of, and I only had to say once at the end that "this young girl was me." Jeff Lane, thank you for always loving me well.

In 2014, it took four hours of tearful prayer to stay vertical as I prepared to share my story with 800 front line leaders from across the nation. When I walked off the stage, a young, business savvy pastor looked at me and said, "How come this is not in book form?" That pastor knew the owner of Lucid Books Publishing, made the connection, and what had been just an idea began to take shape. Pastor Jerrell Altic, you are a firestarter, an insightful businessman, and a man of action. Thank you for investing in so many lives; I am honored to be one of them. And to your wife—Kay Altic—thank you for those hours spent praying and crying on your lap. You are a safe haven for all.

As a busy CEO finding my way, I added a part-time HBU graduate studying for his LSAT to my staff, a young man gifted with excellent project management, organization, and assessment skills, and all the diligence of 20 people put together. Nicholas Van Cleve, I know you will change our nation as a preeminent attorney wherever the Lord leads. I am honored that you chose to spend your time building the base of *Healed for Life*. You are a treasure and fondly thought of always. Thank you.

Hours into my first coffee and conversation at la Madeleine with one of the tallest, kindest men I've ever met, I was struck by God's generosity in hand-delivering a *New York Times* bestselling author to write *Healed for Life* with me. David Gregory, I laud you, your gifts and talents, and am so thankful that you were chosen for this project.

While my oldest child is in heaven, there's a young woman who shares my first's birth year and was grafted into my life through our nonprofit work. Tiffany Pardue, thanks for all the creative strategy in the world—for hearing my heart, refining the vision, and crafting the words as we seek the Lord and build together. Welcome to the Board of Healed for Life Ministries.

Roman, Justice, and Caleb—thank you for your love and maturity in letting me bare every detail of my life to all, often and frequently. You are rock-solid men of God, uniquely impacted by my journey and strengthened for your own. I cherish every moment with you, my miracles and greatest gifts.

Chris, I have always said that God broke off a piece of Himself and tossed it down to me in the form of Christopher Austin Wenz—the tall, dark, and handsome, good Christian millionaire I prayed for, the one who loves God and absolutely adores me, enduring in that love through all my ugly healing years. You, my dear, are the very reason that redemption and our family became reality for me. Your steadfast love is a testimony of what is possible through our Savior.

ABOUT THE AUTHOR

A nationally recognized voice in the Life movement, **Cynthia Wenz** is Founder of Healed for Life Ministries, and champions the healing available to all who have directly or indirectly experienced reproductive grief and loss due to abortion. Having served as President and CEO of a holistic reproductive health center from 2009-2017, Cynthia supports the growth of pregnancy centers across the nation, and has been named one of the Top 30 Most Influential Women in Houston. Cynthia and her Rock-Solid Man of God husband, Chris, live in Houston and have three sons, Roman, Justice, and Caleb.